MARRYING AGAIN

MARRYING AGAIN

The Art of Attracting a New Man and Winning His Heart

Teddi Sanford and
Mickie Padorr Silverstein

CB

CONTEMPORARY
BOOKS

CHICAGO · NEW YORK

Library of Congress Cataloging-in-Publication Data

Sanford, Teddi.
    Marrying again : the art of attracting a new man and
winning his heart / Teddi Sanford and Mickie Padorr
Silverstein.
      p.   cm.
    Includes index.
    ISBN 0-8092-4499-3 : $16.95
    1. Mate selection.   2. Dating (Social customs)
3. Remarriage.   I. Silverstein, Mickie Padorr.   II. Title.
HQ801.S4334   1988
646.7'7—dc19   88-21556
                                            CIP

Published by Contemporary Books, Inc.
180 North Michigan Avenue, Chicago, Illinois 60601
Manufactured in the United States of America
International Standard Book Number: 0-8092-4499-3

Published simultaneously in Canada by Beaverbooks, Ltd.
195 Allstate Parkway, Valleywood Business Park
Markham, Ontario L3R 4T8 Canada

To my husband Don, whose encouragement, inspiration, and love provides the light at the end of every tunnel. He has shown me what a truly wonderful experience marrying again can be.

—Teddi

To all the men I have dated in the past, and to that one special man I have not yet met who will benefit from all the knowledge I have gained in creating this book.

—Mickie

Contents

Acknowledgments

Our thanks to:

Sandra Watt, our literary agent, for her encouragement, enthusiasm, and advice throughout the development of this book.

Shari Lesser Wenk, executive editor at Contemporary Books who believed in this book and nurtured it to publication. We are deeply grateful for her support.

Shalaine Christie, our typist, whose ability to decipher our handwriting and correct our spelling resulted in a professional manuscript of which we were proud.

Our mothers, Lee Schlesinger and Edythe Michael for always being there with love and encouragement through all our ups and downs.

All the men and women we interviewed who were kind enough to share their time, experiences, and deepest feelings with us. A special thanks to Ray Goldstone. Without all of their input, this book would have been impossible.

Introduction

Well here you are, single again, sitting by the phone and waiting for it to ring.

You're back in the dating circus and it doesn't matter if you were married five years or twenty-five years: reactivating your social life as a single woman and finding another partner is not an easy task.

If you're like most women who've been divorced or widowed, especially those who enjoy the familiarity and intimacy of having a permanent companion in their lives, you eventually want to get married again. Your previous marriage (or marriages) may have been wonderful, adequate, or disastrous—it doesn't matter. You now have a terrific opportunity to learn from your past experiences and develop the kind of relationship that will really work for you for the rest of your life.

If you have been out of circulation for more than ten years, be forewarned: the rules have changed.

Competition is much keener. Men have changed. The battle of the sexes is more highly charged than ever. Men and women are suspicious and wary of each other and unsure of how to act or what the other really wants. Don't panic though; the situation isn't hopeless. Once you accept the fact that you may have to reevaluate some of your attitudes and behavior toward men, you can relax and enjoy today's mating game.

We found ourselves in that predicament when, after both being married for seventeen years, we were thrown into the "new" dating scene. We assumed that the rules were the same as they had been the first time around. We thought that if a man said he would call, he *would* call; if he kissed you passionately it meant that he was really interested and would follow up by pursuing the involvement; if he said you were wonderful and exciting it meant the beginning of romance. And we certainly thought that if you went to bed with a man you really cared about, there was no question you were involved in a relationship.

Talk about naive!

We didn't know that:

. . . the feminist movement, as positive as it has been for women in their professional lives, has had a negative effect on male-female relationships.

. . . men are afraid of commitment.

. . . many men are angry and resentful toward independent women.

. . . men are confused as to what role women want them to assume.

. . . many men are bitter as a result of past relationships and costly divorces.

We began to realize that once a woman finds herself single again after a divorce, she must take stock of her attitudes about men and men's attitudes about women, and reevaluate the manner in which she relates to men. A woman who fails to make this transition may sabotage her chances for love and remarriage without even realizing it.

It seems that there is an inordinate number of women who want to connect with the right man and get married again but can't seem to make it happen. So what's the key? Why *do* so many women have trouble making that connection? We've read everything we could find on the subject of men, women, and love. We've found books on why women shouldn't need a man, books that make women feel guilty if they succumb to their yearnings for love and marriage, books that tell women how many rotten men there are out there, books about addictive, compulsive, and self-destructive women. What we couldn't find was a book for women who want to remarry but are uncertain about how to attract the right man in this highly competitive society we live in. So we decided to write a book with a no-nonsense, nuts-and-bolts approach that would realistically spell out the age-old techniques for attracting a man, techniques that have proven successful since the beginning of time.

We began talking to women who seemed effortlessly successful with men, men who were in committed relationships or married to women they loved, men who couldn't find the right woman, women who had happily remarried, and couples who had weathered long-term, happy marriages. We found that no matter what the physical appearance, age, education, or background of the women who were successful with men, there were certain basic similarities in the way they interacted with the opposite sex. They did not deny their basic femininity; they recognized and accepted the biological, emotional, and psycho-sexual differences between the sexes. We started putting our research to practical use in our own lives and noticed that men reacted positively to it. In fact, it worked so well for Teddi that she is now happily remarried!

Since our new personas were working so well for us, we decided to share our knowledge with our women friends. Pretty soon all our friends who were having man problems were calling us and asking us what to do. They would call back later and incredulously tell us that our advice worked!

We realized that we were on to something. So we sat down and wrote out our basic principles. We began teaching courses at an adult education center on the way to attract men, and the response was overwhelming.

The more successes we saw, the more convinced we became that women everywhere could benefit from acquiring this knowledge.

That's how this book came about.

Some of you may have instinctively used some of our program in your past relationships. If so, consider yourself ahead of the game and use this book as a refresher course.

But if you have been unsuccessful in your quest to find love again, if the way you are relating to men isn't working for you, or if you just want some basic, good advice about attracting the right man, this book could be the beginning of a whole new outlook that will lead you to love and marriage again. We hope our formula will be as successful for you as it has been for us and the many other women who have used it.

1
Starting Over

Having been married before, you probably know the pleasures of sharing your life with someone who really cares. You know what it's like to be linked to another person in the closest form of human intimacy. You also know that the world seems to travel in couples—two by two, just like Noah's Ark—and that the single woman is often left out of social activities by her married friends. So, understandably, like most once-married women, you're ready and eager to try again. And as you may have discovered, that's not as easy as it sounds—there are just more of us than there are of them.

It's unfortunate that society has not come up with a better way for mature men and women to meet and mate than the proverbial date, but it seems that very little has changed since we were teenagers. You will either meet a man somewhere and he will ask for your phone number, or a friend will fix you up on a blind date. (By all means, go!) The man will call, ask you out, and pick you up. He will do the driving. He will most likely plan the evening, and he will pay the bill. He will be the one to make the first sexual move.

5

This can be disconcerting to a woman who was safely married to one man for a long time and who thought her dating days were long behind her. However much we might dislike it, it is the process we usually have to go through if we want to remarry, so you may as well learn to do it gracefully.

There *are* men out there, and there are women who will wind up having wonderful, loving relationships with them. Whether or not you will be one of them is very much up to you and how much of an effort you are willing to make. There is nothing wrong with feeling unfulfilled without a man in your life; it doesn't make you desperate or dependent. Readjusting your thinking in order to become more desirable to a man doesn't mean you have to compromise your principles. And there is nothing wrong with using the feminine wiles that have been employed by women for centuries in an effort to attain that goal. The problem is that in the pursuit of independence, many women have forgotten how to use those alluring female charms that have bound men and women together since the beginning of time. Or, once married, we let down our guard and let the techniques we employed to land our man in the first place get rusty from disuse.

So now we have to learn to be captivating all over again. This isn't easy, because to be a successful woman, both in business and in personal life, you almost have to develop a split personality. The same tactics you use successfully in the office are going to bomb socially. We all have to be assertive, outspoken, independent, and strong-willed in certain areas of our lives. But when you are with the man you want, it's a lot more productive (and more fun) to be amusing, flirtatious, and feminine.

If you are a successful, independent woman with nothing to prove (and you should be before you start thinking about sharing your life with a man again), what have you got to lose? Relax, take a deep breath, and enjoy being a woman. There is a significant difference between men and women, and you can make it work for you.

Let's get back to the basics.

Attracting a man involves selling yourself. In practically everything we do in life, from being popular in school, to getting a job, to making friends, to winning an election, we are trying to sell ourselves to others. If you are really serious about attracting and keeping a man consider these basic sales techniques. They're pretty much the same whether you are selling a product or yourself, and they have been used by everyone from politicians, religious leaders, dictators, philosophers, and lawyers, to fashion trendsetters, public relations experts, advertising geniuses, and great courtesans. To make the sale, you must accomplish the following five steps:

1. Get attention.
2. Spark interest.
3. Create desire.
4. Motivate a decision.
5. Stimulate action.

Some people understand and practice the five steps of selling unconsciously, just as some women instinctively practice the principles that attract men. When we buy a product, cast a vote, or choose sides on an issue, we do so because of how persuasive the seller has been, and how he or she has made us feel. The same is true for choosing a mate. A man loves a woman because of *the way she makes him feel.* The women they love may be witty, intelligent, independent, and so forth, but the bottom line is that the women they love make them feel *wonderful.*

Certainly a woman should be successful, strong-willed, self-reliant, intelligent, financially secure, and in control of her own destiny. But a man cares most about how the woman with all those wonderful attributes will respond to him and his needs.

You may have read about the so-called new male who wants his woman to be a complete equal in every way. He doesn't want to be in control, make the decisions, or be a hero to a woman. He is willing and eager to acknowledge his weaknesses and his flaws in order to establish a more honest relationship. Well, don't count on finding one of these new men. If they do exist, they are few and far between. Most men are still most comfortable operating under the old traditional rules. A lot of them won't admit that they still want to be king of the roost, but they do; and the women who understand and feed these needs are the most successful with them. Because after all these years of consciousness raising, feminism, and social upheaval between men and women, now that the dust is finally settling, we have found that nothing much has changed in men's psyches. They may have been forced by legislation and pressure to allow more equality in the marketplace, but they are still reluctant to give up that last bastion of power in their personal lives.

Like it or not, most men want a woman who looks up to them, doesn't criticize them, listens to them, asks their advice, strokes their ego, and makes them feel sexually attractive and like "a real man."

In other words, not much has changed.

We have noticed, however, that one thing *has* changed: the art of romance. Today, the things that previously made a relationship between a man and a woman exciting and fun and special seem to have been discarded as old-fashioned, sexist, dishonest, or silly. In the old days, maybe before most of us were married for the first time, the game of love had its own rules that had nothing to do with the problems, harassments, and disappointments of daily living. Of course, women didn't have to worry about pushing their way up the ladder of success and battling for power in the corporate suites. They were admired and loved for their charm, their gentleness, their flirtatiousness, and their ability to nurture and soothe. It was okay to use obvious ploys like batting your eyelashes, dropping your hankies, and whispering sugar-coated innuendos and vague promises to attract a man. Women played on their own frailty and emphasized the man's strength and ability, using shameless flattery, stretching the truth when necessary to reinforce the male ego, and catering to the man they were after to a degree that would cause the modern woman to shudder in disgust.

They also expected to be properly courted by men. They expected to be treated like ladies, and to be respected and protected. In return, they accepted the fact that it would be their responsibility to make the relationship work. They also knew how to have a pleasant evening with a man without making it a psychological evaluation, a one-upmanship contest, or a gripe session.

Up until the late 1960s or even early 1970s, there was an accepted standard of behavior between men and women. Certainly hormones raged and unwed couples went to bed together, but it wasn't expected or demanded. A "nice" girl could easily hold out for marriage and hang on to her virginity without causing her beau to feel rejected or to run off looking for a more compliant partner. Men were willing to wait, and a woman just didn't have to deal with all the heightened sexual expectations that society has imposed in the last fifteen or twenty years.

The sexual revolution was long overdue for some women, but, like many movements, the excesses outweighed the gains for many others. Before long, men were getting so much "free" sex that they were beginning to demand it before they gave any emotional commitment. Sex and love became blurred, leaving women feeling increasingly unfulfilled and bewildered in their relationships. And because men didn't have to make any commitments to get sex, they forgot what the word *relationship* was supposed to mean. Meaningful communication between the sexes on the subjects of marriage, love, and commitment was difficult to come by.

Now, all this confusion might have been happening while you were safely married, or you might have married in the midst of the changing social and sexual climate. Either way, we want to assure you that the pendulum is once again swinging back to the tried and true basics of love, courtship, monogamy, and marriage. This new climate undoubtedly has been helped along by the advent of AIDS, but even without that threat, relationships were bound to change for one simple reason: most women just aren't comfortable with casual or even steady but uncommitted sex. Most women want love, marriage, permanence, and a husband to love and cherish. So it's up to women to learn (or relearn) the techniques that will get them exactly what they want.

So, here's the good news. You can forget all about your past relationships. You can be as liberated as you want on the job. You can be your own person, develop your potential to the maximum, become financially independent—and still have all the fun and frivolity of being a woman.

Take stock of your attitudes. Approach each new relationship with a fresh view, and we'll give you odds that if you follow our ten-point formula, you again will have a husband by your side to help you over life's mud puddles.

2
The Venus Formula

Our ten-point formula is the most powerful tool in your arsenal of man-pleasing techniques. It is named for the goddess who has been celebrated throughout history as the embodiment of femininity, beauty, and love. Venus symbolizes every man's fantasy of the ideal woman.

These principles are designed to make *you* into a modern-day Venus by showing you how to follow the techniques that men have traditionally found to be irresistible:

1. Make him the star.
2. Avoid arguing.
3. Never criticize.
4. Build his ego.
5. Always listen.
6. Don't complain.
7. Play down your problems.
8. Be vital and amusing.
9. Become sexually uninhibited.
10. Find his emotional key.

11

The ten principles sound very simple. Most of them are based on good manners, courtesy, and consideration of others. Practice the first eight on everyone you meet and you will be surprised at the results. Suddenly, you will be making new friends, both men and women. After all, who wouldn't like to feel wanted, accepted, and worthwhile?

Now you're asking, why do I have to do all this work? Can't I just be loved for my real self? Of course you'll be loved for your real self. But how many times have you thought, "I know once he gets to know me . . ." Sometimes the "real" us just isn't apparent to someone we've just met. We know we're bright, fun, sensible, and interesting, but maybe a stranger sees us as stand-offish or reserved. Maybe we think we're well-informed and articulate, but we come off as argumentative and overbearing.

Dana, a very pretty, stylish, smart accountant, went to a singles dance with her newly divorced friend Jan, who was sweet looking but not nearly as outstanding, well-dressed, or brilliant as Dana. They did the usual look-see over the crowd, and both zeroed in on a tall, well-dressed, interesting looking man a few feet away at the bar; Ron was by far the most attractive man in the room. Both Dana and Jan maneuvered themselves closer and began talking to him. A perfect gentleman, he divided his attention between them equally. Dana, knowing she was far more physically attractive than Jan, secretly assumed that he would eventually choose her. Imagine her bewilderment when, after those few get-acquainted minutes, he asked Jan to dance! The evening was ruined for Dana. She felt rejected and unappreciated, and it showed in her face. All around her, other less attractive women were making connections and having fun, but no man even bothered to approach Dana.

She finally went home, threw herself on the bed, and had a good cry. She had to admit to herself this wasn't the first time this had happened. But she didn't know why.

Let's examine what really happened during those first fateful minutes with Ron. Both women approached *him*, so he wasn't drawn to Jan's looks across a crowded room. Therefore, it was what each woman said, *how* she said it, and the aura she projected that made the difference. Dana had a rather flippant manner, very witty and acerbic. She also had an air of great assurance about her (which some men mistake for haughtiness). Although Ron found her quick wit interesting and she was obviously very bright, he was vaguely uncomfortable with her. Jan, on the other hand, had an open, direct manner, a radiant smile, and a lilting laugh. She seemed soft and warm and genuinely interested in getting to know him. Ron couldn't put it into words, but even though Jan didn't have a great figure, he felt something earthy and sexual about her. He just instinctively liked her and wanted to get to know her better. If Dana had been using the Venus formula, she would have had a better chance with Ron and all the other men she turned off. To some women like Jan, it comes naturally. To others like Dana, it's a learned art.

Men have been socialized to be strong, in charge, sure of themselves, responsible, powerful. They're not supposed to show fears, vulnerability, or insecurity. A Dana-type represents a strong woman who might challenge men and maybe even see through their macho facade. That makes them uncomfortable. A Jan-type represents a woman who is feminine, soft, nurturing, and nonthreatening, able to acknowledge and enjoy men in their masculine role. With

Jan, men feel comfortable and safe. Jan may be just as strong and independent as Dana, but she handles it differently and understands the male psychology better. She can give a man what he needs because she's secure in her femininity and doesn't have to prove anything. Jan also knows that when a man falls in love with a woman with whom he feels safe, appreciated, and comfortable; with whom he can let down some of those defenses he must keep up to appear manly and successful to the outside world; and with whom he is accepted uncritically, he will fight for her, nurture her, and protect her; he will move heaven and earth for her.

Now let's examine each point of the formula in greater depth.

MAKE HIM THE STAR

Men like to command attention. They need to feel important. Very often, deep down, they may feel insecure and less than adequate, but they have been taught not to show it, and they often put on a facade of strength just to prove to the world that they are smart and successful and in charge. A smart woman realizes this and always makes sure that she allows her man to shine. Even the mildest man likes to be center stage with his woman, so let your man be in the spotlight whenever possible. No matter how important and accomplished *you* are, make sure you don't outshine him. Even though you may be the expert on a particular subject, never leave him in the background while you impress everyone with *your* knowledge.

Wrong Way

Susan meets Jack, a mild-mannered, successful accountant. She is a high-powered ad executive who just landed a major account in her specialty area of pharmaceuticals. Her promotion has received a lot of attention within her industry and has been the focal point of conversation at her office for several weeks.

She and Jack have had two dates and are about to embark on their third—to a party given by one of his clients. Neither one expects to know many people there. Soon after their arrival, someone mentions having read about Susan's promotion in the trade papers. That opens the floodgates, and Susan, regularly accustomed to holding center stage at the office, begins to expound on her promotion, the pharmaceutical industry, and the latest drug scandals. She is witty and articulate and holds everyone enthralled.

Cut to Jack, who has just returned from the bar, standing alone on the sidelines holding two glasses of wine. He can't break into the monologue or even get close enough to give Susan her drink. He feels uncomfortable, overshadowed, and unnecessary.

Right Way

If Susan were practicing the Venus formula, she would make him the star. Same scenario—up to the comment about Susan's hot new account.

Then: Susan acknowledges the congratulations with a bright smile. She then purposefully looks around for Jack. Spotting him at the edge of the group holding the two glasses of wine, she walks over to him, thanks him for the wine, and draws him into the conversation. Having found his interests on their two previous dates (point five—always listen), she knows that Jack has other interests besides profit and loss statements. She also knows that Jack is too modest to toot his own horn—it happens that he is a Bonsai expert and has won many prizes for his work.

Susan turns to her hostess and says, "Did you know Jack just won first prize in the Eastern Regional Bonsai Competition?" The hostess is duly impressed and says that she has always been interested in the art of bonsai but has never met anyone with the patience and artistic ability to practice it. As she questions Jack on the subject and he begins expounding on a subject on which *he* is the *expert*, he stands a little taller, his eyes glow, and his arm goes possessively around Susan.

AVOID ARGUING

This doesn't mean you can't state your opinion, make your feelings known, or have a stimulating discussion. But men hate to be wrong, so unless it's a matter of great moral urgency, why waste your time arguing? There are other communication techniques that are nonthreatening: you can state how you feel quietly and pleasantly; you can use humor; you can have a lively give-and-take of ideas and opinions on almost any subject. But if your man is really steamed up about *his* opinion, and you can't come to an agreement, just let him have the last word. *You* know where you stand, and *he* knows where you stand, so why press your point?

This does not mean that you shouldn't stand up for your feelings and desires in your personal relationship—of course you should. But even there, it's usually pointless to argue. It's much more effective to state your position plainly and firmly without getting into long, drawn-out discussions that only turn into arguments. You have a right to your opinions, a right to your needs, and a right to your feelings. If you let your man know this and understand it yourself, then what is there really to argue about?

In the beginning of a relationship, arguing is self-destructive and self-defeating. In a social context, particularly, insisting on the last word and making someone uncomfortable and angry is a turn-off. If you must engage in heavy debate, choose your subjects carefully. You may win the argument and lose the man. Obviously, if you continue to state your opinion and he completely ignores your feelings, this may not be the man for you. But if your goal is to move ahead with the relationship, then think twice before you get on the soapbox.

Wrong Way

Janet and Bill are out with another couple. They are discussing the state of the economy. Bill is a trial lawyer who, although he's bright and witty, sometimes has a know-it-all attitude. He is raving on about the dire state of the economy, the irresponsibility in Washington, and the fact that the unemployment rate is the highest since the Depression. Janet has just read exactly the opposite in *Time* magazine. She turns to Bill and says, "Bill, for a lawyer you certainly don't have your facts straight." She then proceeds to quote *Time*.

Bill's face turns red, and he bristles as he tries to defend his position in front of their friends. An argument ensues. Bill is increasingly angry, and everyone is embarrassed and uncomfortable. Mentally, Bill vows never to date that "aggressive, bitchy, know-it-all" again.

Right Way

Same scenario, different approach.

When Bill expounds on the economy, Janet responds in a pleasant, nonthreatening, nonabrasive tone, "I agree that a lot of people feel the way you do, Bill, but it's interesting that this week's *Time* took the opposite view." She never said he was wrong, nor did she challenge him directly, but *indirectly* she let him know there *is* a different point of view on the subject.

Janet sees clearly that no matter how much she may disagree with Bill, his opinion of the economy and the media has nothing whatever to do with their personal relationship. Therefore, she diffuses the situation by smiling sweetly and saying, "Who knows what the future holds? I wish we all had a crystal ball." She then proceeds to ask him about the big case on which he is working, and the situation is neutralized.

NEVER CRITICIZE

There is no such thing as "constructive" criticism. No one wants to hear their faults detailed "for their own good." If your man asks for your opinion on touchy subjects, weigh your answer carefully and stress the positive. If there is something about him that irritates you or that you want to change, think long and hard before you mention it. Chances are, he knows about his irritating habit and either can't or won't change it. He will not appreciate hearing about it again from you.

You *can* make many changes without ever resorting to criticism. If you don't like his ties, buy him a couple of new ones and ask him to wear them especially for you. If he needs a wardrobe makeover, take him shopping and enthuse over the clothes that make him look good. Most men want to please their woman, and the more you act in a positive manner, the more he will try to accommodate you.

If a man treats you in an unacceptable way, don't criticize him directly; simply tell him how his actions affected *you*, and request that he not act in that manner again because of *your* feelings.

Finally, never criticize someone or something that can't be changed. If he picked out an inappropriate gift for your birthday, bite your tongue and say you love it. If he shows up in the wrong outfit on the wrong day for the wrong party, throwing a tantrum won't change things. You might as well accept it and see the humor in the situation.

Wrong Way

Erica and Tim are going to a black-tie affair. He arrives wearing an outdated blue ruffled dress shirt with his tuxedo, which he has rented especially for the occasion.

As she greets him at the door, he gives her a big hug and says, with a self-satisfied smile, "How do I look?"

Erica looks obviously disappointed and says, "How did they talk you into that tacky ruffled shirt? They haven't worn those in years."

Tim is crestfallen. The evening is over as far as he is concerned. The hours of preparation Erica has spent painting, powdering, and planning to be sexy and alluring are to no avail. Tim can't wait for the evening to be over.

Right Way

Same scenario, but when Tim asks how he looks, Erica spins him around and tells him how wonderful and sexy he looks in the tuxedo. She would die before mentioning that his blue shirt is all wrong. After all, he is already wearing it and he can't go home and change, so what's to gain by criticizing his appearance and starting the evening off on a negative note?

Even if Tim had specifically asked Erica if the shirt was okay, she would not have criticized his choice once he was already wearing it.

Sometimes a little white lie is acceptable.

BUILD HIS EGO

This is *very* important, possibly *the* most important principle in the Venus formula. Men have very fragile egos. There is no man on earth who is impervious to compliments. Tell him how wonderful he is at every opportunity.

If he is a sportsman, his stroke, stamina, drive, serve, and coordination, are absolutely awe-inspiring. If dancing is his thing, you've never been so in-tune with the music in your life. If he is proud of his work or has won an award or a bonus, make a big occasion of it and be sure to let everyone know how great he is. If he helps little old ladies on the subway, tell him how much you admire his manners and sensitivity. If you look, you will find all sorts of things to compliment your man about. And it is *very* hard to resist someone who really thinks you're wonderful.

Men also love to impart their knowledge to women, so if you could ask him to teach you how to do something he's expert at, he will be delighted to oblige. And never, ever, be better at it than he is!

You can even turn a potentially negative situation

into a positive one by a little judicious ego stroking. And when it comes to sex, flattery will get you everywhere. A man's ego is most vulnerable in the bedroom, so concentrate your efforts on complimenting his sexual prowess.

Wrong Way

Helen and Bruce have been going out for several months. Now they are in bed together for the first time. Both have the usual first-time jitters.

When the lovemaking is finished (to no one's great satisfaction), there is silence until Bruce finally says, sheepishly, "I guess it was too quick for you." Helen shrugs, smiles wanly, and says, "It was okay. Don't worry about it. It will be better next time." She then gets up and disappears into the bathroom.

Bruce is so humiliated by her obvious lack of enthusiasm, he has already decided there won't be a next time.

Right Way

Same couple in bed. As often happens the first time, Bruce isn't the great lover for whom Helen had hoped. But Helen realizes the pressures on men to perform. She also knows that how she handles this will make or break the future of their relationship.

Even though Bruce makes no reference to their unsatisfactory lovemaking, she senses that he needs reassurance and immediately compliments him. She can't say that the act itself was wonderful because Bruce knows better than that. But she can and does tell Bruce how smooth and wonderful his skin feels, how his mouth really turns her on, how warm and sensuous his body feels against her, and so on. She will rave about the entire experience rather than dwelling on any less than perfect aspects of it. Bruce suddenly begins to feel it *was* a wonderful experience and is eagerly looking forward to the next time, when he *will* fulfill both their expectations.

ALWAYS LISTEN

The way to a man's heart is through your undivided attention. If he feels that what interests him interests you, he will find you fascinating.

There are many tried and tested listening techniques you can use to show your undivided attention. Always look directly at your man while he is talking to you. Make eye contact as often and as long as possible. Ask pertinent, short questions at appropriate breaks in the conversation. Do not interrupt. Let him finish his thought before you elaborate on yours. Men interrupt women much more frequently than the other way around (and men often are poor listeners), yet *they* complain that women talk too much!

It's sometimes frustrating for a woman, but if he makes it up in other ways, what's the difference? You're not going to change him, anyway. What you are going to do by employing active listening techniques is show that you think he is a fascinating, interesting human being. Lean forward, show enthusiasm and interest, and listen intently. He will think you're wonderful.

Wrong Way

Cathy and Earl are on their first date. In addition to being very attractive, Cathy makes a good living in a "man's field," mortgage banking. She is also an excellent conversationalist. Earl is a stockbroker who has a tendency to talk too much when he's with a woman he wants to impress.

All through the evening he regales her with stories about his clients, his travels, and his opinions on everything. She attempts to keep up her end of the conversation and vivaciously matches him story for story. Although Cathy is intelligent and charming, Earl (for reasons he doesn't understand) begins to feel vaguely annoyed. "Why do women have to talk so much?" he thinks to himself. He begins to withdraw and the evening becomes increasingly uncomfortable. Cathy senses she will never hear from him again, but she doesn't know why.

Right Way

Same scenario. Earl is doing most of the talking. Cathy understands the importance of listening, so she smiles, gives him her undivided attention, hangs on his every word, and asks appropriate follow-up questions, which lead him to expound even more. After a while, he begins to see that she likes him, that he doesn't need to impress her. He begins to ask *her* questions, and before long, they're having an equal conversation.

By the end of the evening, Earl is convinced he's in love. He makes another date immediately and tells Cathy she is one of the most intelligent and interesting women he has ever met. Cathy smiles knowingly to herself. She knows she's playing a game and she's winning.

DON'T COMPLAIN

Bitch to your girlfriends, if you must, but when you're with a man, try to take things in stride and be easygoing. Men can't stand women who whine, nag, get overly upset, and nit-pick about every little thing.

Complaining is a nonproductive activity that doesn't accomplish anything except annoying your partner. Most men turn off completely when a woman complains about anything. To them, a complaint is a form of nagging, whining, and bitching— all traits they abhor in women. Even when your complaint is directed at an inanimate object (e.g., it's too hot outside, you have a headache, the restaurant is too expensive), somehow men tend to take it personally and are sure the complaint is really directed at them.

When a complaint *is* justified and necessary, don't be accusatory. State your case calmly and emphasize how the man's action made you feel. And if he doesn't change his actions to please you, then either accept him as he is or find another man.

Obviously, this is different from complaining when you are dissatisfied with a business or service transaction, in which case aggressive complaining will probably accomplish wonders. But love and commerce are very different sides of life. The same man who fields complaints all day at work has no patience for them from his date that night. He just wants to relax and enjoy himself.

Wrong Way

Mike has chosen a new Italian restaurant for his second date with Nancy. During the course of the evening, a few things go awry. Mike passes up the valet parking, requiring Nancy to walk four blocks in her flimsy high-heeled sandals. She moans about the bumpy sidewalk and the thin soles on her shoes. The restaurant is crowded, and Mike forgot to make a reservation, necessitating a forty-five minute wait.

She spends the time tapping her foot impatiently and looking at her watch. Their table is near the kitchen and under the loudspeakers. Nancy looks irritated and upset every time the waiters brush by her, and she complains about the music. When the menu is offered, she looks at it briefly and announces that everything is too spicy or too fattening. The restaurant is hot and smoky, and the waiter is rude. Nancy points these facts out to Mike.

They get through the evening somehow, but it is the last one they spend together.

Right Way

Same scenario, but Nancy walks the four blocks holding Mike's arm for support and privately thinking she can always soak her feet when she gets home. She practices her listening skills on Mike while they wait for a table. She doesn't usually eat Italian food, but she lets Mike suggest and order, figuring a few bites won't kill her. She knows that the restaurant is hot and the waiter is rude but realizes she can't change that, so why make Mike feel even worse? She seems to be having such a good time that Mike is enchanted—he thinks Nancy is terrific for being such a good sport and is already planning their next date.

PLAY DOWN YOUR PROBLEMS

Don't bombard him with your financial, emotional, career, and family troubles. He may not be reluctant to discuss *his* problems, but he really doesn't want to have to deal with yours, even though he may ask.

In the beginning of a relationship, a man wants to be entertained, soothed, and delighted by his woman.

He wants to think she is beautiful, happy, bright, and charming. He wants to fantasize about her romantically and sexually. He really doesn't want to know anything negative about her or her life at this point. He's not emotionally involved with her, and he has plenty of his own problems; he certainly doesn't need to be burdened with hers. It makes him feel uncomfortable and slightly guilty, as though he should be doing something about them. Many newly divorced or widowed women make the mistake of dumping their anger and/or grief on a man. Don't do it.

Most men will quickly run away from a woman they perceive as problem-ridden. Because a man is brought up to believe he has to be strong and solve problems, subconsciously he will feel that she wants him to solve hers. There are some men who are rescuers and who are drawn to needy women, but most men aren't, so don't take the chance of driving away a terrific man by dumping too much on him too soon. Of course, once your relationship is more steady, you should certainly feel free to share your life and your problems. But in the early stage, find someone else to tell your troubles to.

Wrong Way

Polly has had a really bad week. She did not receive the promotion she had counted on at work. She has made the painful decision to put her mother in a nursing home. Her son may be on drugs, and she has just received word from the IRS that she's being audited. Fifteen minutes before her third date with Ray, her dishwasher backed up, flooding her kitchen. She has barely mopped the kitchen and dressed herself when Ray arrives, punctual as usual.

Ray is greeted at the door by a disheveled Polly

whose first words are, "My God, I should have known you'd be on time." Ray looks uncomfortable and taken aback. Polly manages to get herself together and the evening proceeds, although she's clearly distracted. When Ray asks her about her promotion, she launches into a tirade about her boss, her company, and their lack of appreciation for her work. Ray is even more uncomfortable. She half listens to his attempts at conversation, and when he comments on her distraction, she apologizes and immediately presents a litany of her other problems. By now, Ray is completely disenchanted and wants to escape. After all, she's not the only one with problems—he has plenty of them, too, but she never gave him the chance to air them.

Right Way

Same date . . . same problems. Ray arrives on time, and Polly manages to seem ready and eager to see him. When he asks how she's been, she smiles and answers, "I've been better, but things are looking up now that you're here."

During the evening, he inquires about the promotion. Polly dismisses it lightly, saying it hasn't come through this time. She doesn't mention any of her other disasters, figuring there is nothing that Ray can do about them, so why burden him with all her problems? And when Ray tells her about his rough day at the plant and his run-in with the foreman, she is sympathetic and consoling. By getting her mind off herself and on to Ray for the evening, she finds herself relaxing and enjoying his company. Tomorrow her best girlfriend will get an earful of Polly's troubles, but for tonight, life is just a chocolate milkshake.

Polly knows that in a later stage of a relationship she will share some of her problems and feelings with Ray, but she also knows that everyone has problems and no one, except your mother, your husband (or long-standing lover) or your best friend really wants to hear yours.

BE VITAL AND AMUSING

If you are energetic and are turned on to life, you will draw men to you like a magnet. Men want to be soothed and amused. Be flirtatious, upbeat, and enthusiastic and learn the art of light conversation.

Men are attracted to upbeat women. Many men are shy or uncomfortable in purely social settings and are grateful to a woman who puts them at ease and makes conversation easy for them. Always have a few amusing stories or a couple of topical jokes at hand to help ease the conversational flow. If you have a funny joke to tell about yourself, go right ahead—as long as he will find it amusing.

Learn how to ask open-ended questions so he will be forced to answer with a whole thought. Don't ask, "What did you think of the last Woody Allen picture?" Ask instead, "What do you think is the appeal of Woody Allen?" Or ask who he thinks will win the World Series. Pretty soon he'll be chattering away and enjoying himself immensely.

Always know some interesting, offbeat, or amusing places to go on a date with him if he asks you for suggestions. Many men are quite unimaginative in their dating habits and would welcome a change of pace. But always be sure he will be comfortable on new turf. You want him to feel relaxed, refreshed, and revitalized when he's with you. No matter how difficult your day was or how tired you are, psyche yourself up to be smiling and fun.

Wrong Way

Kelly has had a hard day at work and would like nothing better than curling up alone in bed with a good book and a TV dinner. But she has a blind date with Zack, who has been highly recommended by her good friend. She thinks to herself, "Oh, it probably won't work anyway. Blind dates never do. I'm so exhausted, I'll just let him carry the ball." Because of logistics, she has to go straight from the office to meet him at the restaurant. She doesn't bother to change from her business suit, and perfunctorily freshens her makeup. Zack is already there when she arrives.

The maitre d' escorts her to the bar where Zack is waiting. She smiles wanly and offers a limp handshake. She projects an air of indifference and seems colorless and listless. Zack feels uncomfortable and tense. Is she disappointed in him? Doesn't she feel well? Has he turned her off in some way? How is he going to get through the evening, he wonders.

Right Way

Same tired Kelly, except this time she changes from her suit to a silk dress she has brought with her. She redoes her makeup carefully, fluffs up her hair, and adds some festive jewelry and a big splash of her favorite cologne. Already she feels better. She mentally shifts gears, telling herself, "I know this is going to be a great evening—I deserve it after the day I've had!"

She arrives projecting self-confidence and vitality. She greets Zack with a warm smile and a firm handshake, telling him flirtatiously how much she has looked forward to this evening and how happy she is that her friend got them together. Zack is immediately charmed by her warmth and enthusiasm, and the evening is off to a great start.

PRACTICE SEXUAL SURRENDER

This is a subtle form of mentally letting go during sex—flowing with the feeling and mentally opening your mind and body to the delights and sensuality of lovemaking with your man. Sexual surrender transcends technique. It encompasses all your senses working together to transport you and your partner past the purely physical to a higher level of emotional rapport.

Psychologists refer to a feeling known as the *state of flow*. It happens when you are operating at the peak of your abilities, so engrossed in what you are doing that you feel an incredible energy flow or high. Time and place fade away. Your concentration on the moment is complete and intense. As you let yourself go and give yourself fully to your partner, a mutual energy flow will pass between you. The intensity of the experience will transform it from a mere act of sex into a feeling of complete emotional and spiritual oneness. You both will feel incredibly close to each other. Concentrate on the skin, smell, feel, and presence of your man, and revel in the pleasure of your mutual contact. Forget for now positions, techniques, or perceived inadequacies. Just let the moment wash over you.

Wrong Way

Liz and Ralph are making love. Ralph is doing his best to please her, but Liz's mind is far away on the speech she is giving tomorrow. She has always prided herself on her sexual responsiveness, and so she goes through the motions automatically. She has already decided she is too distracted to have an orgasm, but she figures at least she will satisfy Ralph by participating vigorously and faking it.

What Liz didn't realize was that a sensitive man like Ralph realized instinctively that Liz was with him in body only. Even though Liz was a technically expert lover, Ralph felt unsatisfied and somehow cheated. He never called her again.

Right Way

Same scene. Liz forces all other thoughts out of her mind and allows herself to concentrate on the pleasures of the moment. As they make love, Liz mentally and physically lets go and allows herself to revel in the sensuality of Ralph's mouth and body entwined with hers. Before she knows it, all thoughts of tomorrow have completely evaporated, and she feels more passionate as he senses her total involvement. Liz doesn't have to fake orgasm; the power of sexual surrender sweeps her to fulfillment. Ralph is overwhelmed by the intensity of their lovemaking and feels closer to her than he has to any woman in a long time.

FIND HIS EMOTIONAL KEY

Every man has deep, hidden emotional needs. If you can discover the way to meet those needs, you will be rewarded by his undying devotion and love.

Some men need to be mothered. They have a strong need to be nurtured and babied, but they would die before they would admit it or ask for it. Some men have deep inferiority feelings and actually want a somewhat bossy, take-charge woman to shape them up. Some men have deep-seated sexual desires that some women might dismiss as "kinky," while others are willing to accept and cater to them. Some men are starved for love, attention, and affection but don't know how to show it. Some men need to be needed. Others need to need you. Some men are adult little boys; others are father figures. Some want a clinging woman; some need lots of privacy and space.

You cannot find a man's psychic key on the first few dates, but they all have one. Keep your eyes and ears open as you get to know each other better. Follow all the points we've been describing, and very soon' your man will feel comfortable with you and begin to let down his emotional barriers. As you get closer, he will reveal (perhaps obliquely) his secret center. Once you understand and uncritically accept the very core of his being, you will also have his love. If he trusts you with his soul, he will surely trust you with his heart.

Wrong Way

Ruth and Nat have been dating steadily for six months, and she wants that final commitment. On the surface everything appears fine between them, but somehow the relationship seems to be at a standstill. What Ruth doesn't know, because she hasn't picked up the signals, is that Nat, while admiring her self-sufficiency, really wants her to be more dependent on him. His mother, who he adored, was semi-invalid, and although Ruth knows his history, it has never occurred to her that he has a deep-seated need to be a caretaker. Ruth prides herself in handling all life's exasperating details without asking for help. She's efficient, and she can handle most things with a minimum of effort. She brushes off Nat's attempts to take over some of the details and thinks he will appreciate her more if she doesn't seem needy.

Nat feels there's something missing in the relationship. He's extremely fond of Ruth, but the kind of feeling that leads to permanent commitment just isn't there for him.

Right Way

Ruth has listened carefully to Nat's fond memories of his mother and his reminiscences of the wonderful emotional rapport he shared with her. Many men would have considered the pressures of caring for an invalid mother a burden, but Ruth realizes that Nat enjoyed the responsibility. Obviously, it fulfilled a deep-seated emotional need in him. Ruth, who is a very capable and independent woman, is sensitive and intuitive enough to ask Nat's advice in many areas that she could handle herself because she is aware of his need to be protective. She solicits his opinion on choosing a new car, which money markets to invest in, even what to serve for dinner. He responds by spending more and more time with her.

The night her son is rushed to the hospital with a burst appendix, Nat is the first one she calls. When he arrives, she rushes weeping into his arms. Nat feels a sudden surge of protectiveness and love. One week later, he proposes.

PROJECTING THE VENUS AURA

We all know women who seem to have no trouble attracting and captivating men. They are not necessarily great beauties or super achievers, nor do they possess perfect bodies. Yet when these women enter a room, they somehow project a powerful magnetic aura that draws men to them.

A few lucky women seem to possess this power naturally, and although this magnetic allure is difficult to define, you know when someone has it. Whether you call it charm, charisma, sex appeal, personality, vivaciousness, self-confidence, mystery, or whatever; the Venus aura is all these things, but every woman has her own way of projecting it.

Myra is a Princess Grace type—tall, statuesque, and regal looking, with sleek, short blonde hair. She has a soft southern drawl, and there is a calmness about her that makes her easy to be with. Even though she is a successful businesswoman, Myra doesn't talk a lot. What she does is *listen* and ask questions. Don't think that her presence isn't felt in a discussion, because it is. She expresses her opinions and contributes intelligently to a conversation, but when she isn't expressing her views, she is giving her full, undivided, and rapt attention to the person to whom she is talking; she always appears vitally interested in what the person is saying. That seems only polite and a matter of common sense, doesn't it? But next time you are in a group, look around and see how many people actually do it. Do *you*?

Myra has also been described as having a mysterious and rather elusive quality about her. Although she is warm and expresses herself well, she stops before you really get to know everything she thinks and feels. She leaves you wanting more and feeling eager to be with her again.

Myra told us about one evening she spent with a man. They went out for a long, leisurely dinner during which her date talked a great deal about his business, his sports accomplishments, and his children. Myra let him take center stage, while she listened intently, made the appropriate acknowledgments, and smiled a lot. At the end of the evening, the man complimented her profusely, telling her that she was one of the most intelligent women he had ever met and that he couldn't wait to be with her again.

Carolyn is another example of the power of that special aura. She is the complete opposite of Myra in physical appearance, with a mane of thick, curly, dark hair, worn au naturel, and huge, soulful, clear blue eyes. She has a warm but somewhat shy personality, and she too projects an underlying calmness, almost an ethereal quality. She is soft-spoken and very direct in her manner, and her friends say that when she talks to them, it's as if no one else exists. They feel as if she has genuine empathy for their feelings.

Carolyn met her husband through a video dating service, and he says that he still doesn't know what caused him to select her out of all the videos he saw. He had always dated tall, blonde, athletic types with extremely outgoing personalities and a sharp wit. He saw plenty of those on the video tapes, but there was something special about Carolyn's aura (and he used the word *aura*) that touched him in a new way. He wanted to get to know her better and find out what was behind that mesmerizing gaze.

Another example of a woman with a special aura is Doris. She is central casting's stereotype of the girl next door, with red hair, freckles, and about ten pounds more than she would like to have. Doris is always exercising and dieting but she is still slightly heavy. She knows how to minimize her extra inches with the right clothes, and her few extra pounds have never mattered a bit to men. She has always been the most popular girl in her class, her sorority, her office, at parties—anywhere she goes. She always has a smile on her face, radiates confidence, and never looks bored. She is an outrageous flirt with every man she talks to, whether he's the grocery clerk or her husband, and she does it with such grace and charm that other women aren't threatened by her—they like her as much as the men do. She is a good listener with everyone, including children. She has a direct gaze and knows how to express more than just words with her eyes and the tone of her voice. Despite her open, friendly manner, Doris gives the impression that there is a lot more to her than meets the eye. Men and women alike want to get to know her better so they can find out what's underneath all that effervescence.

Doris met her husband on a tennis vacation for singles in the Bahamas. Every available woman in the group was after him, but Doris was the one he gravitated toward. She had to leave the cruise early to return to her job, and although most women would have been worried about leaving him there with all those other women on the prowl, Doris knew that she had already worked her own magic and that he would remember it. He did. They have been happily married for many years, and she is still enchanting him with that special aura.

The three women we have described are all quite different in looks and personality. But they are also alike in many ways. They are all good listeners, they hold back just enough of themselves to give an air of mystery, they use their eyes and voice and body language to communicate, they are easy to be with, they focus 100 percent on the person they're with, and they make the most of their assets.

Developing your own wonderfully seductive aura is the first step in attracting a man. You will find that it will also improve your relationships with people in general because they will be drawn to you in a positive way.

The most important key to projecting the Venus aura is first to truly like and feel comfortable with yourself. We can't emphasize enough that before any woman sets out again to find the right man, she should be sure she is the right person for *herself*.

Then, learn to use your eyes, voice, and body language. A large majority of the men we interviewed said the first thing they noticed about a woman was her eyes and the way she used them. Many women have completely enchanted a man without even uttering a word just by a seductive stare across a crowded room or a promising look across the table at dinner. You can say maybe with your eyes even when you are verbally saying no. Your eyes can also send signals that you are unapproachable even though your conversation may be charming and flirtatious. Your eyes can say that you are afraid, angry, bored, unsure of yourself, or nervous—even though you are verbalizing the opposite. We have yet to meet a man who isn't flattered and charmed, at least temporarily, when a woman looks deep into his eyes and smiles. After a while it will become second nature to know how to make eye contact with a man and hold that contact for just the right amount of time.

Your voice can be a very powerful tool. Its tone and inflection can completely change the way what you're saying comes across. Have you ever met someone on the phone and found yourself completely enchanted by the sound of his voice? Well, a beautiful, sexy woman's voice can have the same effect on a man, as evidenced by what happened to Larry. He had just moved to New York and wanted to reach an old buddy. When he called the number he had been given, a woman answered and said his friend had moved. They struck up a conversation on the phone, and he immediately began to envision her: tall, blonde, sexy, completely his type. He was so enchanted by her voice that he asked her out for the next night. He received quite a surprise when she opened the door: she weighed more than three hundred pounds—definitely *not* his type. It was their first and last date, but at least the woman had the opportunity to get acquainted with a new man.

As for body language, there have been dozens of books written on the influence of body language on a person's image. In fact, about 55 percent of what we communicate comes from body movements and facial expressions. If you have poor posture and a hangdog expression on your face, then you are communicating a very negative message that says, "Don't bother with me; I'm not worth it." If your face reflects every negative emotion you feel, make a conscious effort to control it. If you're bored with what someone is saying, use your will and your facial muscles to look pleasant and alert. And don't do it only with men; everyone likes to see a happy person.

To learn to use your eyes, voice, and body to communicate warmth and sexuality, buy yourself a notebook and write down what you observe about women who seem to effortlessly draw men to them. Also write down everything you can remember about *your* actions on your last date or the last party you attended and how others reacted to you. You'll probably be surprised at what you did and didn't do. Once you learn how people react to you, you can change their reactions.

Let's talk for a minute about flirting—not the obvious, salacious kind but the old-fashioned kind women used to do behind fans. Whatever happened to that wonderful art? Men loved it and women had a great time doing it. It doesn't have to mean an invitation to bed—it's just a moment's total attention exchanged between a man and a woman, a reminder of the wonderful possibilities that exist between the sexes, and a subtle promise that something special could happen. Women who have mastered the fine art of flirting are very seductive and appealing. They also have a lot of fun.

There's another element that's essential to projecting the Venus aura: the observance of courtesy and good manners. It's amazing how many attractive, bright women destroy their image by being rude and exhibiting bad manners. Men are embarrassed by this. If a man hears you being rude to waiters, service personnel, and others you feel are unimportant, it will lower his opinion of you—no matter how rude or abrasive he may be himself.

Teddi learned this on a double date with another couple before she and her husband were married. The other man, Andy, was someone they had gone out with before, and Teddi was always uncomfortable with the rude manner Andy used with service personnel. She didn't know his date, Farra, but it soon became apparent that Farra had as little regard for the help as Bob did. She was extremely rude and insensitive, never saying thank you and speaking to the waiter in an abrasive manner. Strangely enough, Andy was relatively polite and very quiet for a change. A few days later, Andy mentioned that he was disgusted by Farra's attitude and lack of manners and that he wasn't going to see her again. Farra probably wondered why she never heard from him again, even though she was attentive to him and the evening seemed to be successful.

In addition to observing standard good manners

and common courtesies, keep in mind that there's nothing wrong with encouraging and accepting traditional behavior from men. There is a primeval protectiveness that men feel when opening the car door for a woman, helping her with her coat, lighting her cigarette, walking on the outside of the sidewalk, and just generally acting as a buffer between a woman and the small abuses of everyday life. We have found that the feminist movement has generally left men confused about how to respond to women in situations that would traditionally call for these small courtesies. Most of the men we spoke to admit that they consider women who expect to be treated in the traditional manner to be more feminine. Many of them also said that when they could sense a woman was accustomed to that kind of treatment, they tended to treat her with more consideration in all areas.

It may seem a little awkward to stay in the car for that long minute while he gets out, locks his door, and walks around to your side. He may even assume you're going to hop out on your own, and he'll be halfway down the block before he realizes you're not beside him. But just stay put and eventually he'll get the message. Remember, you're special. You're not one of the guys. You're used to being cherished. Now, you may think it sounds corny and old-fashioned, that it's ridiculous not to do these things for yourself when you are perfectly capable. However, arousing a man's protective instincts can be very appealing to him. It will also make you feel wonderful, and once you become accustomed to being treated like the special person you are, it will become part of your persona, as natural as breathing. Your seductive aura will be the essence of your femininity and the center from which you project your personality.

NONE OF US IS PERFECT

No matter how good our thoughts and intentions, we all have those moments when we say or do something that we regret. After all, we're only human. When this does happen, there are some sure-fire techniques for correcting any mistakes you feel you might have made and dissolving any potential disasters in your relationship.

Several years ago, a group of us was going to a charity event and had gathered for drinks beforehand at Sue's house. Her date, Max, was a little late so everyone was already there when he arrived. When he came in wearing a navy suit, it was apparent that Sue had forgotten to tell him it was a black-tie affair. The first words out of her mouth were, "You can't go like that. Where is your tuxedo?"

Poor Max looked distraught as he reminded her that she hadn't *told* him it was formal. Since he lived on the other side of town and it was already late, he couldn't go back and change. Several people jumped to his defense and said it was no problem—there were always a few men without tuxedos at every ball. Max looked miserable but laughed it off and decided to make the best of it.

In the meantime, Sue had had second thoughts about her tactless remark and the effect it would have on their future relationship, which she wanted to develop. She knew she had badly embarrassed him and if she didn't do something to rectify the situation, he would probably be uncomfortable all evening, have a miserable time, and never call her again. So, right before our very eyes, she transformed herself into an entirely different woman, apologized for her "dumb" remark and told him he would be the best-looking man at the dance, no matter what he wore.

Then she proceeded to devote herself to making him comfortable, getting him a drink, fixing him a plate of hors d'oeuvres, drawing him into the conversation, asking his opinion, and subtly directing the conversation to a recent local tennis tournament he had won. In other words, Sue made him the center of attention in a positive way.

She continued to focus her attention on Max for the entire evening. At the ball, she never left his side. When some of the other men at the table asked her to dance, she declined, saying that her dance card was reserved for Max. She made it a point to introduce him to everyone she knew, and made him feel that she was very proud to be with him and considered him to be very special.

Her behavior had a double effect on Max. It compensated for the embarrassment he felt about wearing the wrong clothes and also allowed him to relax and have a good time. And it put him slightly off-balance because Sue was normally a rather cool and reserved type. Her attentiveness and flirtatiousness intrigued him, and he wondered which was the real Sue. In fact, it intrigued him enough to continue dating her, and that led to their present arrangement—marriage.

You can also dispel the ill effects of a disagreement by using humor. Teddi does this frequently with her husband when they have political arguments. Their views are quite different and they are both very vocal in defending their positions. Occasionally, their political debates get too heated and take on a tone of personal attack. When Teddi feels this happening, and realizes that the situation has passed the point of logic or calm reasoning, she starts poking fun at both her views and his, and shows that they're both being ridiculous. If this kind of game playing offends your sensibilities, just keep in mind that there are very few subjects worth causing a rift between you and the man you love. The self-satisfaction you gain from not backing down is a nice feeling, but, to most women, it runs a poor second to loving and being loved by the man of their choice.

No matter how hard you try to avoid it, sooner or later you will probably lose your temper (and more than once) if you are involved in a relationship. Just try to make it later than sooner, and keep your priorities in mind.

Playfulness is another way to smooth over those troubled times. Women have had to maintain such a delicate balance with the men we love that we sometimes forget the fun and freedom of being playful and carefree. Make a concerted effort to inject some playfulness into your personality—lighten up and don't take yourself so seriously. This will be particularly effective if you are usually the serious, no-nonsense type.

One of the women we interviewed for this book told us how she put the magic back into her relationship when she sensed it needed a boost. Diane is a busy executive and very conservative and tailored in her appearance. But there is another side to Diane behind that proper facade. Whenever she realizes she's been grumpy, irritable, and generally unlovable with her boyfriend, she plans a special surprise for him the next time they're together—something completely out of character and just pure fun.

The last time it was a picnic in bed surrounded by candlelight, with his favorite X-rated film in the VCR for dessert. She wore a filmy pink teddy and the pearls he had given her for Christmas. The next day she was back in a business suit, but you can be sure there was one man sitting in his office who still remembered her in pink satin and pearls.

Of course, there will be times when you've had a bad day or are just in a rotten mood. This isn't going to drive away any man worth your time. No one demands perfection—especially if they are being made to feel wonderful most of the time. If you do something that you truly regret, though, it never hurts to send a cute card, a flower, or maybe a balloon to his office, where he can enjoy the reactions from his coworkers. No need to go into lengthy apologies; he'll get the message. Then let him make the next move.

We should explain that there is a difference between forgetting to use the Venus Principles and injecting a little spice into your relationship by an occasional eruption of temper. If the foundations have been firmly set, and you can maintain control of your emotions, a temper flare-up can add some excitement and sexual tension to a relationship. If you don't instinctively know how far to go with a tantrum and how to do it with style, don't do it. It's not something you can easily learn; some women just know how to do it. No matter how hard you try to avoid it, sooner or later you will probably lose your temper (and more than once) if you are involved in a relationship. Just try and make it later rather than sooner, and keep your priorities in mind.

THE VENUS CHECKLIST
How to Capture His Heart . . .

- Be generous with compliments.

- Take more than a passing interest in his work. Learn about it, be able to discuss it intelligently.

- Listen actively. The ability to be a good listener is much more important than a gorgeous face or body.

- Be selective about what you tell him. Don't talk about being unfaithful to past husbands or lovers. Don't dwell on physical, financial, child-rearing, or business problems.

- Ask for and take his suggestions and let him know you did.

- Think of unusual fun things to do.

- Let him teach you things.

- Surprise him occasionally with small presents or funny cards.

- Always exhibit "class". (i.e., If you borrow his car, refill the tank before you return it; if he asks you if you need money for clothes, groceries, etc., say, "No, but thank you so much for asking.")

- Baby him. Men love women who "mother" them— not "smother."

- Be on time.

- Let him think he's the boss.

- Retain some mystery.

- Be flirtatious.

- Compliment him in the company of others.

- Have a sense of humor.

- Learn to enjoy things he likes. You may find that activities you had never even considered trying are fun, i.e., spectator sports are boring unless you understand the game, but once you do, they become a whole new experience.

- Let him do the pursuing. Men like the "chase" and they lose interest if there is no challenge.

. . . and Keep It!

- Don't ask him, "When am I going to see you?"

- Don't tell your friends (or his friends) intimate details about your relationship.

- Don't be too intense. Intensity can be exciting if it's properly channeled, but it can be overpowering and a turn-off if there's too much of it in the beginning.

- Don't have sex before the relationship is established in other ways.

- Don't try to force a relationship that you know isn't right for you.

- Don't ask him out more than once unless he follows up by asking you out again.

- Don't tell long stories about people he doesn't know, gossip about trivia, etc. . . . it's boring.

- Don't interrupt. People who are good listeners are involved in what they are hearing and know when there is a natural opening for a question.

- Don't tell him your inner fears and psychological hangups.

- Don't put down his ex-wife or other women he knows, even in teasing.

- Don't get into heated arguments on any subject. An exchange of ideas or even a debate does not have to become an argument. When it does, it usually becomes personal.

- Don't spend too much time talking about your kids.

- Never criticize him in front of others (or alone, for that matter).

- Never call him just to chat.

- Don't call him at work unless it's absolutely necessary and then make it short.

- Make a special effort to get along with his children.

- Don't borrow money from him—ever.

- Don't hint about things you would like him to buy you as a gift.

- Don't make long distance calls on his phone.

- Don't talk about commitment.

- Don't tell him about other men who have treated you badly.

3
How Do You Measure Up?

Pretend for a moment that you're a man. Would that man be interested in getting to know you? If he entered a room full of people and was introduced to you, would he be attracted enough to want to spend more time with you? Or pretend you see yourself walking down the street. Would you think, "Boy, I would like to look like that"?

As much as we would like to believe that it's not true, we are judged, at first anyway, by the way we look—especially by men, and in most cases, even by women.

Sure, there are many women who could be considered overweight or unattractive and are married to wonderful, loving, successful men. But if we're talking about first impressions here, why not create the best image you possibly can? Now that you're single again, you'll find that there's a lot of competition out there; when you look and feel your best, others can't help but notice.

There is considerable evidence that the number one thing that first attracts a man to a woman is good looks; the more attractive a woman is, the better chance she has of appealing to men. No one likes to hear this, let alone believe it. We would all like to be noticed and loved for our inner beauty, sensitivity, intelligence, and various other wonderful qualities. Unfortunately (or fortunately for those lucky enough to be born natural beauties), most men are still hoping to win the prom queen.

The good news is that beauty is truly in the eye of the beholder, which is why some men fall victim to tall brunettes and others grow weak at the sight of a petite blonde. The secret is to make the most of your own personal assets and to use all the tools available to encase your wonderful qualities in an attractive package. Every woman has the potential to do this, but it may require a little time, effort, and money. It will be the best investment you can make.

Just keep in mind that before you can overwhelm a man with your charm, charisma, wit, sensitivity, compassion, and sparkling personality, before you can employ the power of the Venus formula, even before you can lock in that first date, you have to get him to at least notice you. And chances are that a lot of other single women are trying for that same second glance, because as we know, there are a lot more of us out there than them.

No one says you have to be a candidate for a Playboy centerfold, but with today's technology and cosmetology there is absolutely no reason that every woman shouldn't look attractive from head to toe. There have been ten zillion books written on how to do it. There is every kind of makeup to correct every kind of flaw, there are department stores and beauty salons full of consultants who will show you step by

step (and for free) how to become a new you. There
are fashion consultants by the dozen who will coordi-
nate and accessorize you. There is no end to the
incredible cosmetic improvements available to
women—and yet we are constantly amazed at how
many women do little, nothing, or the wrong things
to enhance their natural attributes.

There are a few basic truths that hold true for
almost all women over thirty—and for many who are
even younger. They are:

• *Just because it's "in style" doesn't mean it's for you.*

Sometimes it seems the fashion industry is con-
spiring against women. But there are plenty of mir-
rors around, and we should all have enough common
sense to know or to ask whether or not we look good
in four layers of baggy clothes, tight toreador pants,
fanny wraps, mini skirts, or any of the other fashion
gimmicks that burst upon the fashion scene every
year.

If you're unsure about what looks good on you,
drag along a friend when you shop (the one who will
tell you when you look terrible). Then be sure you
don't buy anything that doesn't make you feel like a
million bucks!

• *We all could use a little makeup.*

We went through the early days of the feminist
movement, when we were told that men showed their
real faces to the world so women shouldn't hide
behind a false image by using makeup—it was dishonest. Baloney! Makeup is truly the eighth wonder
of the world. It can transform almost any face and
make its owner feel special. Even when the no

makeup edict was in, we always believed in helping nature along. In fact, we wouldn't stray too far from home without at least some blusher and mascara.

However, be careful not to overdo it. You can't cover wrinkles and bags with heavy makeup—it just makes them more evident. The older you get, the more subtly your makeup should be applied. Heavy eyeliner and rouge emphasize what you are trying to minimize. We have a friend in her fifties who will never admit her age—which is okay. But she was once a model, and she still wears the same makeup that looked great on her when she was a cover girl, complete with false eyelashes. The effect is almost a caricature, and it's a shame because underneath all the pancake makeup she is a beautiful woman. One morning Teddi stopped by her house to return some books and caught her without her war paint. She looked fifteen years younger.

The astronomical rise of the cosmetics industry proves that more women are learning about the magic of makeup. You can bet that men wish they could share in some of that magic to disguise their five o'clock shadows, cover up their gray hair, darken their eyelashes, and give their cheeks a healthy glow—and more and more of them do just that, as evidenced by the skyrocketing sale of men's cosmetics.

- *Gray hair, no matter how attractively styled, makes you look older.*

There is no reason to let your hair go gray unless you are playing a grandmother in a movie. If you are extremely young looking, a silver streak or a frosting of silver in black hair is dramatic. And there are those few fortunate beautiful women who look great with silver flecks in their hair, no matter what age. For most of us, though, it doesn't work. *There is nothing wrong with looking as young and fresh as possible.* When it comes to attracting men, looking young is a plus, like it or not.

- *You are not going to look your best if you are overweight.*

We're not talking about five or ten pounds. But if you are more than ten pounds overweight, you probably have lumps and flab that don't look good in or out of clothes. Moreover, most women don't feel good about themselves if they are overweight. If you don't feel good about yourself, why should anyone else feel good about you? Self-confidence is a very attractive quality in men and women, and it is much easier to feel and project it if you like what you see when you look in the mirror.

- *If you need surgical help to look the way you want to look and you can afford it, go for it.*

It's a good investment. It will certainly last longer than a fur coat, a cruise, or a new car. You may not be able to fool Mother Nature, but you can fool just about everyone else with cosmetic surgery. This goes for cosmetic dental work, as well.

It is true that cosmetic surgery is expensive, but it can be financed if necessary. Not everyone feels the need to take ten years off their face or have a perfect set of teeth, but if you have that desire, don't feel guilty or foolish about it. *You* are the best investment you can make. New cars, clothes, jewels, or even a man won't give you the Venus aura unless you feel wonderful about yourself. Of course, a younger look-

ing face, capped teeth, or lifted eyes can't do it all, but
for some women, these things can be that final boost
that brings it all together.

- *Experiment with new looks.*

Remember the old movie cliché? The straightlaced
secretary wore her hair in a bun, horn-rimmed
glasses, and menswear gray suits with sensible shoes
until one day after working late, her boss looked into
her eyes, gently removed her glasses, pulled one pin
from her long, lush hair, and she was transformed
into a starry-eyed seductress with whom he immediately fell in love. That fairy tale plot may be
slightly exaggerated, but there are those women who
have "reinvented" themselves, thanks to their own
efforts, *not* those of Prince Charming.

One of them is Nellie. She had been married to a
doctor for thirty years when he decided that time was
passing him by and he needed to "experience life"—
with another woman. Nellie had always been a nice
looking woman, though somewhat subdued, maybe
even a little plain. Her brown hair was tinged with
gray, and her tailored suits were always in good taste.
After a year of feeling sorry for herself, Nellie decided
that she had better start experiencing a little bit of
life herself and that maybe she should do it with
some new wrapping. So she colored her hair red, got a
permanent, deepened her blue eyes with blue contact
lenses, spent four hours with a makeup consultant,
invested in a new wardrobe of stylish clothes, some
of which were decidedly sexy. Suddenly, she had more
confidence than ever before, as everyone raved about
her new look.

Even if you don't go as far as Nellie, try to change
something about your look every so often. Reinvent-

ing yourself can have a stimulating and brightening effect on your entire personality. So if your current "self" hasn't been working for you as well as you would like, try one or all of the following:

• *Change your hair color or highlight your hair.*

This is a wonderful way to give yourself a lift. One woman we know reversed the old adage that blondes have more fun. She was a rarity—a natural blonde—and she was very sexy looking, even without trying to be. She is one of those women who had always had her choice of men, but she felt men didn't take her seriously or appreciate her intelligence, either in her profession or personally. So, one day she dyed her hair a rich chestnut brown. She claims that from that day on, she no longer projected the image of a glamour girl, and people began to take her more seriously. Granted, most women don't have the problem of being *too* glamorous, but you can do a lot to change your image with a new hair color.

• *Get a new hairstyle.*

One of the biggest mistakes women make when it comes to their appearance is keeping the same hairstyle they had for ten, twenty, or thirty years. What looked great on you at twenty may not have the same effect at forty.

• *Reorient your wardrobe.*

If you have always been the tweed-skirt-and-sweater type, put a little spice in your closet by adding to your wardrobe some trendy items and accessories that you wouldn't normally wear. Study fashion magazines and observe the women whose images you admire. Most of the department stores have fashion consultants who can help you develop a new fashion image little by little. Even if you are the tailored type, put some touches of femininity in your wardrobe. It doesn't have to be ruffles and bows, but men love feminine clothes on a woman, and you will find that you *feel* and *act* much more flirtatious and appealing if you are wearing something feminine.

Blatantly sexy clothes outside the privacy of your own home (or his) are a negative. Even the men who are turned on by seeing a woman in sexy, cleavage-revealing outfits are more comfortable if she doesn't overdo in public. True sex appeal is not blatant or overstated. One of the sexiest women we know never wears anything low-cut or tight fitting. Her clothes are always understated and simple, but she always wears wonderfully spicy perfume and a fresh camellia somewhere on her outfit. We can't figure out where she gets them when they are out of season, but she always does. She almost never wears jewelry except for diamond ear studs (they could even be cubic zirconias, for all we know), and she always wears high heels, even with her perfectly tailored blue jeans. And she is always surrounded by men at parties, even though she is happily married.

- *Broaden your interests.*

Sit down and make a list of the things you would like to learn more about, perhaps art, music, theater, dance, urban planning, architecture, religion, politics, or the environment. Then set forth a plan to become educated in those areas. If you decide on art, for instance, visit all the local museums, start browsing in small galleries. Talk to the gallery owners, ask questions, read up on the artists whose work you particularly enjoy. Make it your business to know who the upcoming young artists are, and learn to recognize their work. In other words, become well-versed in the areas of your interest so you can discuss them intelligently. Your new-found knowledge will not only make you more interesting, but you'll meet lots of new people who share your interest.

• *Try something you've never done before.*

There is nothing drearier than a person who is stuck in a rut and refuses to take a chance on a new experience. Loosen up and let yourself enjoy new sensations, whether they involve trying exotic foods, taking up golf, or going up in a hot air balloon. An enthusiasm and excitement for doing something new and different is very appealing, and it will make you a much more interesting person.

A business associate of ours who is about fifty-five told us that she was stuck in a rut, bored with her life, and beginning to feel her age. She had gotten to the point where she actually panicked at the thought of changing her routine. We convinced her to make a list of ten places in Los Angeles (her hometown) where she had never been, ten foods she had never tried, and ten restaurants to which she had never been, and to give herself one month to do all of these things. She agreed, reluctantly, but she did it. Of course, trying new experiences didn't give her a complete new outlook in one month, but she did open up her life, met some new people, and found there were lots of things out there that she could enjoy once she made herself try them.

• *Lighten up your personality.*

One of the things we have noticed about women

who come to our seminars and classes is that a lot of them take themselves too seriously. Everything has psychological overtones and has to be analyzed to pieces; everything has to be "meaningful" and "significant"; everything is an issue or a problem. This kind of outlook can make everyone feel and act old. The fact that you're single again may mean that you've gone through some tough times, but if you try to exhibit a more carefree attitude about life and its inconveniences and disappointments, you won't feel and act like you have the weight of the world on your shoulders.

- *Allow yourself to be playful.*

Playfulness is a charming characteristic of youth whether you are six or sixty years old. Teasing, cajoling, and acting silly occasionally are fun and free the spirit wonderfully. A playful woman attracts people of all ages to her because she is fun to be around.

- *Go through your wardrobe and throw out everything you wouldn't wear if you thought you would meet someone you wanted to impress.*

Sure, you can save a few things for when you're washing windows or painting the kitchen. But you get the general idea—get rid of the clothes that make you feel and look anything less than your best. You never know when "Mr. Right" is going to appear.

- *Start exercising, if you don't already.*

Force yourself to walk upstairs instead of using the elevator. Walk to the store instead of driving. Park a mile away from your destination. Join an exercise class of some kind. Guaranteed you will feel better as well as look better, because a trim figure will make you look younger and healthier.

• *Never let a day go by without reading at least one newspaper—and we mean* all *of it, including the sports page.*

This is not just so you can wow people with your knowledge of current events. You will feel much more confident and comfortable if you are familiar with the subjects that people around you are discussing, and you can contribute to the conversation. Keep in mind, though, that you don't ever want to sound like a know-it-all. There's no need to take center stage to impress people, especially a new man. Let him know that you recognize his expertise and knowledge; he'll let you know how much he appreciates it.

• *Try to learn about at least one spectator sport.*

Most men really go bananas over women who understand and enjoy sports. We know a man who had dated practically every gorgeous woman around, and ultimately chose to marry a woman who has an almost fanatic love of sports, especially baseball and boxing. She was also bright and beautiful, but he swore that the thing that first intrigued him and led him to want to spend lots of time with her was her love of sports. Sure enough, she could rattle off all the major league scores and knew the vital statistics of every world boxing champion for the last thirty years. This kind of dedication may be more than most of us can handle, but at least try to remember what game they play in the World Series and who won the Super Bowl.

● *Learn how to cook at least a few things well.*

There is something about a woman in the kitchen that turns a man on. A man feels nurtured when a woman cooks him a good meal; it reminds him of his mother, and you know how most men are about their mothers. It is also a nice way to show your appreciation to a man who has taken you out a number of times. It'll give you a chance to get better acquainted in a setting you can control.

ADVICE FOR THE "SEASONED" WOMAN

Let's face it, like it or not, fair or unfair, men *are* attracted to younger women. But you can overcome that handicap and fool Mother Nature by projecting an ageless aura, no matter what your age. Much of how our age is perceived by others stems from the way we think of ourselves. If you *think* of yourself as past your prime, then you will act old and look old. If you think of yourself as young and vital and conduct yourself as if age is of no consequence, you will retain an aura of youth. A seasoned woman who projects the Venus aura can be very provocative and suggest a special mystique that only comes with time and experience.

We met a woman at a party a few years ago who personified what we're talking about. She was standing with a group of people, mostly men. She gave the impression of being tall, but on closer inspection, she was only about 5'2" and slim. She was dressed all in white with a long white chiffon scarf around her neck. Her makeup was perfect but very subdued, her hair was long and red. A very handsome young man was standing next to her with his arm around her waist in a proprietary manner. He was talking at the time, but she was so animated and radiated so much vitality that it was she who held our attention. *Her* attention, however, was on him—completely—and the sexual current between them was evident. We found out later that the woman was sixty-seven years old. Her husband, the young man she was with, was thirty-four. They have been together for ten years. Sure, she looks older than he does, but there is something so electric about her that you don't even notice that, biologically, she could be his mother. Of course, this is an extreme example: most sixty-seven-year-old women can't get away with long, flowing red hair and don't have any interest in marrying a man half their age. But it does point out that age is a state of mind and that agelessness can be achieved regardless of what the calendar says.

The woman we described hasn't had a facelift or any other cosmetic surgery, but that is an option you may want to consider. As we've said, if you will feel better about yourself and have more confidence by lifting and tucking away a few years, go for it. But don't think that just erasing the years from your face will automatically make you ageless. Only your attitude can do that.

We know one woman who, after getting a divorce at age forty-eight, found herself experiencing several unsuccessful attempts at developing a new relationship. She decided a facelift might be the answer, and anticipated having to practically beat men off with a stick when she came out with her new face. She was bitterly disappointed when she realized her luck with men wasn't improving. Her face was smoother and firmer, but her persona hadn't been operated on. And the bottom line is always what's behind the face, no matter how beautiful and young that face may be.

So keep in mind that it's not just the package, but what you do with it. If a man senses an underlying sensuality and earthiness in a woman, her age becomes irrelevant. In Europe, older women have always been appreciated for their experience and charm. They are considered to have a *savoir-faire* that is sought out by men of all ages. Many of the great courtesans have been well over forty, but neither the passage of time nor the pull of gravity decreased in any way their ability to enchant and delight the men of their choice.

All women, once they pass a certain age, are at one time or another faced with that age-old dilemma—to lie or not to lie about their age. We find that most women feel it's to their advantage to lie a little, and there's a good reason. Ideally, we should be allowed to age gracefully and wear our years proudly as a badge of living. However, if you're going to be practical and face reality, the reality is that this is still a youth-oriented society. Therefore, women who feel their age is an impediment should shave off a few years. You can level with your man later after he has had the opportunity to get to know you, and by then, he won't care.

One circumstance when it might be a good idea to lie about your age is when friends are offering to fix you up with a new man. Many times we have attempted to match up single women friends in the forty-five-plus age bracket with men of the same age or older. Our initial description of the woman makes the man enthusiastic about the meeting, but invariably, if he asks her age and we level with him, he sheepishly proclaims that he usually dates women in their thirties (or younger).

So we knock off a few years, and no one has ever complained of misrepresentation. In fact, one match that we take credit for involved a sixty-year-old man who was notorious for dating only women under forty. We introduced him to a friend who is fifty-four years old, and so what if we rolled back the calendar fifteen years. She is a terrific woman with an ageless persona and a good understanding of how to please a man. After six dates, she told him her true age—and by then he wouldn't have cared if she were seventy. They recently got married.

Do use common sense and your mirror to determine the lowest age you can feel comfortable with. One woman we know, with the help of a little minor surgery and a photocopy machine, managed to stay forty-seven until she was sixty-five. She even changed her birth certificate and her driver's license by whiting out her age, substituting the birth date of her choice, and photocopying the documents. She slipped up, though, when she went to Europe with her boyfriend—she forgot to do her passport—but by then he was so crazy about her that she was able to convince him the passport bureau had made a mistake.

Most of us aren't going to go to those extremes, but just remember that age is only a state of mind. So if you happen to ignore a few years in order to have the opportunity to show a man how wonderful you are, why not? In the long run, he will be glad you did.

If you are over forty-five, it is likely that the man you want is at least forty-five or older. If so, you'll get great results from the Venus formula. The older a man gets, the more he is conditioned to expect traditional behavior from a woman and the less tolerance he has for what he considers aggressive women.

Older women are very often more comfortable in this role, and therefore are able to project that certain very appealing mystique that comes only with time and experience.

Let us reiterate that by *traditional* we don't mean subservient or dependent. In the traditional male-female relationship, the woman provides an oasis where the man is soothed, emotionally stroked, and made to feel important, needed, and admired. Biologically, men need to be dominant and aggressive and they prefer their women to be soft and receptive rather than high-powered and assertive—at least in their personal relationships. Social conditioning in recent years has moderated this drive in some younger men, but it is still there lurking under the surface. Most men over forty want to be the boss— even though they may be "liberated"—and they respond positively to a woman who at least gives them the illusion that they are in control.

Older men are particularly sensitive to any behavior that threatens their male conditioning. Many of them are going through emotional and physical transitions that further threaten their egos. They have tremendous fear of losing their virility and sexual capacities, which are emotionally tied to the male concept of dominance. All of these psychological factors intensify as a man grows older, and a woman who understands these needs is much more likely to gain his love and commitment.

No matter what your age, the crucial thing to remember is that while you can easily make a good first impression, it's the magnetic power of your personality that is the real key to keeping a man.

Don't make the same mistake often made by beautiful women of relying solely on your physical attributes to attract men. Beauty may cause a man to notice you at first, but there is always another beautiful woman just around the corner. It's the way he *feels* when he's with you, not a perfect figure and a flawless face, that will keep him by your side permanently (although an attractive package makes the discovery of what's inside even more exciting!).

Rose is a good example of what can happen if you depend too much on your outer image and overlook what's inside. After only two years of marriage, her husband had divorced her to marry a woman ten years older and not nearly as beautiful. Rose kept belaboring the fact that she had worked at keeping her appearance exactly as it had been when they had first met and that he had always been so proud of her beauty. She felt she had been the perfect wife and claimed she would never understand what went wrong.

Her husband, though, made it quite obvious what went wrong. It was true that he had been dazzled by her beauty and proud of the way other men looked at her and envied him. He admitted that he had been so flattered that such a beautiful woman would want to marry him that he was blinded to her negative characteristics, which included selfishness, egotism, a desire to always be the center of attention, a lack of sensitivity and warmth, and an obsessive concern about her appearance. After a few months, the thrill of his beautiful possession began to wear off, and by the end of a year she didn't even look that great to him. Meeting the other woman was his way of correcting his mistake.

You don't want to get to the point where you've concentrated so much on your exterior that you've

overlooked the interior. There's little doubt that a
man will base his first impressions on what he sees,
but his second and third impressions will be based
on the "real" you he comes to know.

VENUS INVENTORY CHECKLIST

- Is your figure as good as it could be?

- Have you emphasized your best features?

- Is your hairstyle appropriate for your age and image?

- Do you follow the basic rules of nice appearance?
No unkempt hair, chipped nail polish, run-down
heels, runs in pantyhose, slip showing, poorly fit-
ted or completely outdated clothes, peek-a-boo bra
straps.

- Is your perfume subtle and not overpowering?

- Do you read the newspapers and a news magazine
regularly?

- Can you laugh at yourself when necessary?

- Are you easy to be with?

- Have you learned to flirt?

- Are you aware of the signals you give through
body language?

- Do you always maintain eye contact when speaking to someone?

4
Understanding the Male Mystique

A women who is successful with men is one who understands their psychology and acts accordingly. There *is* a difference between men and women. It doesn't matter whether this difference is biological or environmental. The fact is, it is there, and we women must recognize it. Warren Farrell, in his book *Why Men Are the Way They Are*, states: "The male primary fantasy is to have access to as many beautiful women as desired without risk of rejection. Women's primary fantasy is commitment, security, and family."

So when a woman marries, she has attained her fantasy, but when a man marries, he has actually given up the attainment of *his* fantasy. Therefore, if we accept this premise and follow it to its logical conclusion, it's easy to see why men don't easily commit to marriage.

Frankly, we think this is a rather simplistic view of

men and women, but we do agree with Farrell and
other psychologists, sociologists, and students of
human behavior that men have a built-in fear of
intimacy and of losing control. Men have not been
socialized to accept their feelings of love, fear, rejection, jealousy, uncertainty, happiness, tenderness,
loss, and so forth the way women have. And they
certainly have not been encouraged to verbalize
these feelings. Imagine a man calling his male
friends for an hour's conversation about what happened on his date last Saturday night, including who
said what to whom and how he felt about it the way
women do. Men have been taught since childhood
that any such displays of emotion or uncertainty are
unmanly. Men have been taught that they must work
hard, earn money, be responsible for their families, be
strong, not cry, fight wars, be the sole or main sup-
porters for their families, and stay in control. They
are never supposed to feel insecure, vulnerable,
afraid, or rejected. Of course, that's impossible. Men
do feel all those emotions, but instead of acknowledging and accepting them, they often repress them.
Often, the male "tough guy" pose is really a cover-up
for insecurity. Little wonder that women complain,
"Why can't men articulate their feelings?", "Why are
men afraid of commitment?", "Why are men so insensitive?", "Why does he get so upset, so angry over
nothing?" Men are that way because they *are* vulnerable, but are afraid to admit it to themselves. They
often *are* insecure or afraid of rejection, but don't
want to acknowledge those "weaknesses." For many
men, it's easier to just run away from the woman who
evokes those unwanted feelings.

A man both needs and fears a woman. He wants
desperately to be loved and accepted by her, but he's
also afraid she might weaken or ridicule him. He

both wants her and wants to *not* want her. This duality of emotion drives women crazy unless they understand it. It explains why so many men run away or pick a fight or do something else to upset the relationship just at the point where it's beginning to become emotionally intimate. That's when you really have to go into high gear to reassure him that while you love him and adore him, you're not going to smother or entrap him.

From a man's point of view, he *does* face rejection every day. He faces rejection at work. He is the one who usually initiates a date by asking a woman out; if she chooses not to go, he is rejected. He is usually the one to initiate the first sexual move; if the woman says no, he is rejected. Ask any young teenage boy how it felt the first time he summoned up enough nerve to corner that dream girl at her locker and ask for a date or the first time he called her on the phone. If she laughed at him or turned him down, he probably wished the earth would open and swallow him up. With each success a man grows bolder, but each rejection sets him back again.

Women, too, face rejection, but because we're socialized differently, we handle it more openly and understand its limits. We can deal with it better because we're encouraged to talk and cry and express our hurt.

While single women probably have it much harder than single men overall, and while it's sometimes hard to sympathize with men and *their* emotional problems, the fact remains that if you don't understand a man's feelings and motivations, then you won't be able to handle him effectively, and in the end you'll lose out on what we're all looking for: love.

Men, by nature and instinct, need to be the aggressors, particularly in sex. That doesn't mean that once established in a relationship you can't initiate love-making. Actually, you should, quite often—it's good for a man's ego to know you want him. But during the sex act itself, sexual expression is a biologically aggressive act to a man. We all know that there is no consummation of the sex act unless the man has an erection, making him the initiator. A woman, by nature, is the receiver. This difference is very profound, and a wise woman will accept and encourage the polarity of masculinity and femininity.

To a man, his sexual organ represents an overwhelmingly strong sense of power. A very good male friend of ours told us how he felt as a young boy masturbating for the first time. "I saw that giant thing rise up and throb in front of me. It was almost as if it was a disembodied organ separate from my body, pounding and pulsing away. I was awestruck at the power and pleasure available to me by just touching that odd-looking part of me. It was almost as if it had a life of its own. The knowledge of what I could make it do made me feel strong and powerful. I don't think a woman can ever fully understand what the power of his penis means to an adolescent boy and, even later, when he becomes a man."

Yet, in spite of its power, the penis is also a fragile instrument that doesn't always obey its master and rise at will, particularly when the man is trying to make love to a woman. So, in spite of the importance men place on the magic powers of the penis, they are always afraid (sometimes only subconsciously) that it is going to let them down at a crucial moment. A woman who doesn't understand how fragile a man's ego is when it comes to his sex organ can't know men at all.

We didn't understand the complexities of male sexuality when we were young brides. Like most women of our background, we were fairly inexperienced in the deeper mysteries of sex and assumed our husbands would know all about the art of love. It never occurred to us that, while they may have been technically experienced, they had no more knowledge of what pleased a woman than we did. And we really didn't give a thought to what male sexuality means to a man and how wrapped up it is with his entire personality. It was something we learned many years later.

A woman's sexual drive is not the all-powerful, pervasive force that it is in a man. We don't have an external organ that so urgently needs release. Our sexual feelings are more diffused and, while they might make us uncomfortable if they're not relieved, they are usually not as urgent as a man's. This biological fact accounts for much of the difference between men's and women's actions. Men's urge to fight, some criminal behavior, their competitiveness at sports, and many of their aggressive drives stem from the hormonal, biological, and anatomical differences between men and women. Until you understand and accept these differences, you will never understand men.

There are some men who really adore women. They understand them, relate to them, empathize with them. These men always have many platonic female friends, and at a party they invariably choose to talk to the women rather than the men. These aren't the Don Juan types, or womanizers, who basically think of women in sexual terms for gratification of their egos. You can discern the types pretty quickly because the Don Juans exclude a subtle sexuality that, while it usually attracts a woman, also makes her feel slightly off-balance. The man who truly likes women is simply interested in you because you're a woman. He'll notice your clothes, your new hair style, your jewelry. He's interested in your job, your kids, the latest gossip. He's charming to women of every age, and women adore him right back! Lucky is the woman who lands this kind of man for herself.

Mickie was lucky enough to have a love affair with one of these rare men. Right after her divorce, she met Kevin, who had also been recently divorced. He was from a big, close, Irish Catholic family and not only was he the oldest child, he was the only boy among six sisters. His sisters looked up to him, vied for his attention, spoiled him. He, in turn, was protective, and affectionate toward them, basked in their adoration, and felt as though he had his own harem. Because there were so many women around all the time, Kevin was used to female paraphernalia, female emotions, female bodies, female scents, female everything! He watched his sisters cope with their first menstrual periods, their first dates, their first love affairs. When they fell down, he dried their tears. He listened to them giggle with their girlfriends. He was their confidant, their mentor, their friend, and their role model. Sometimes he became annoyed at having so many laughing, crying, talking, squabbling, noisy women around, but mostly he found them fun, lively, pretty, and more complex and interesting than his boyfriends.

As he grew older, Kevin found that it was just as easy to relate to other girls as it was to his sisters. He instinctively understood women. He made love instinctively, too, and was open, loving, and sensuous. He delighted in a woman's curves, smells, skin, hair, being. Kevin could be a woman's friend as well as lover. He could talk "girl talk," gossip about friends and strangers, share his deepest fears and fantasies. He even liked to go shopping! But don't think for a minute that he was a wimp. Kevin was a college boxing champ and a ranked amateur tennis player. He could drink with the best of men and was thoroughly masculine. But unlike most men, he was not afraid to give in to his softer side, and because he didn't fear women, he had no trouble falling in love. In fact, Kevin couldn't imagine *not* being in love. To him, a woman by his side to love and protect was as necessary as food and drink. Less than a year after Kevin and Mickie's romance ended, he married someone else. Mickie's affair with Kevin was not fated to become permanent, but it showed that there *are* men around who truly like and need women, and who are unafraid to acknowledge it.

HOW MEN VIEW WOMEN

But most men are much more ambivalent than Kevin toward women, due to their early experiences with their mothers. A typical little boy's first memory of a woman is of his mother, toward whom he has many mixed emotions. She was the first person he bonded to as a baby. She nurtured, held, loved, and fed him. She kept him warm and dry. As he grew up, she wiped his tears, nursed his cuts, and calmed his fears. That's the good part he remembers—the nurturing part. But as he grew up, it was his mother who also scolded him, corrected him, set limits on him. Sometimes his mother was unhappy and cried, and that made him feel guilty. Sometimes his mother relied on him too heavily to be her "little man" and that made him secretly resentful, and then, again, he felt guilty. Sometimes his mother yelled a lot, but rather than be a bad son and yell back, he kept his resentment inside. No matter how much he resented his mother's control, he still went to great lengths to protect and care for her. He loved and needed her, while at the same time he tried to pull away from her.

By the time he is grown up, the man has collected these ambivalent feelings toward his mother, which he then subconsciously transfers to his feelings about all women.

Now, of course, men do fall in love, make commitments and get married. Obviously, your husband did. But they do so *in spite* of their unresolved feelings toward women. The woman who is successful with men understands men's fears and knows how to put them to rest. She understands a man's vulnerability and fear of rejection and his feeling that marriage means responsibility and obligation. She recognizes a man's deep fear of commitment and doesn't push too hard while at the same she is becoming emotionally indispensable to him.

So what does a man really want from you? He wants to feel comfortable with you. He wants to know you like and approve of him. He wants to feel he can trust you and that you take him seriously. He wants to be understood, respected, and appreciated. He wants to be needed by you. Even a man who says he wants a strong, independent woman really wants a woman who's somewhat dependent on him in some area. It makes him feel important, and feeling important and being right is life's elixir to most men.

Have you ever met a man who will admit he's lost or stop to ask for directions? Men will drive around for hours, never quite admitting they don't know where they're going. They will backtrack, go around in circles, and justify every wrong turn rather than admit they're lost. Women, on the other hand, will stop to ask directions, make a phone call, or do whatever is necessary to get where they intended to go as quickly as possible.

Men and women just think differently. They approach problems differently, handle emotions differently, react to stress differently. It may be inherent or it may be cultural conditioning, but what's the difference? The point is, that's the way it is, and a wise woman will recognize these differences and accept them. So, the next time your man is lost, you're thirty minutes late for the party, and you're ready to scream, "Stop the car, you idiot, and go phone to find out how to get there!", just take a deep breath. Keep your cool, shut your mouth, and let him play out his scene. When you finally do arrive, he will try to make it up by being so attentive and charming to you, you'll be overwhelmed. It's his way of recognizing that you let him off the hook, didn't nag or belittle him, and left him with his ego intact. He'll never, ever admit he was wrong, but he *will* be grateful that you didn't point it out.

Men don't like to fail at anything, whether it's maintaining an erection or rebuilding their car's engine. They need to feel they are invincible, especially around the woman they love or want to impress. Our friend, Jan, learned this the hard way. She had dated a man a few times who she really liked, and she was hoping that this budding relationship would turn into something serious. He was a computer whiz and loved to putter around fixing up his house. He bragged to Jan that he had completely rewired and replumbed his house and was now making new furniture for it. Following that clue, Jan asked him to fix her dining room chandelier, which had mysteriously stopped working. In exchange, she would fix him a gourmet dinner. Bob accepted eagerly, saying that it would be an easy job, and Jan prepared for a romantic evening, figuring it would take Bob just a few minutes to fix her light fixture.

Well, of course, it didn't work out that way. After disconnecting her large and heavy chandelier and plopping it in the middle of her living room floor (on her white rug), Bob found that the wiring was just a little more complicated than he thought. He struggled with it for more than an hour, growing more frustrated by the minute. Jan was distressed and suggested several times that Bob just leave it. She apologized profusely for getting him into something so complicated, but by that time it was a no-win situation for both of them. Bob was embarrassed that he couldn't get it to work right and became more determined than ever to fix it. The harder he tried, the more his ego was on the line. By this point, Jan was helpless. In *his* eyes, Bob had failed her. The fact that it didn't matter to Jan—that she still liked him anyway—didn't register with Bob. It mattered to *him*. He finally gave up, but the evening was ruined. Bob was hot, sweaty, and angry at himself. He just picked at his dinner in a state of distraction. He soon left, promising Jan that he would come back later in the week to complete the job properly. She never heard from him again. Finally, Jan called him; he gave a lame excuse about working night and day and promised to call just as soon as this "rush job" was finished, but, of course, he never did.

At first, Jan was dismayed at losing Bob over something so stupid. Then she was hurt, and finally, angry. After all, the jerk had left her with a chandelier in the middle of the floor. Not only that, but it cost her a small fortune to fix it. The electrician she finally called told her the wiring had been all messed up by Bob's ineptitude (and Jan added, his ego).

Granted, this may seem like an extreme case, but more than one woman has experienced something like it. The simple truth is that most men cannot stand being caught in a mistake or appearing to be inept, and they would rather just leave the situation and pretend it never happened than have to admit defeat. Naturally, this can drive women crazy, so you'd probably be smart not to put your new man to the test. Bob and Jan did not have a long history together. Their romance was only a few dates old, and it clearly wasn't worth it to Bob to try to save face; it was easier for him to just drop the whole thing and start over with someone new.

The moral is, don't ask a man to do anything for you right away, especially if it's something you're not sure he'll succeed at. On the other hand, if he *offers* to help you out and it's something he knows well, let him (remember, Bob didn't offer to fix the light fixture, Jan asked him). We've had men help us buy cars and tires, move furniture, drive us to airports, fix the plumbing, take us to and from hospitals. But either they have offered, or we were involved enough with them to be able to ask for their help.

EVERY MAN'S FANTASY

You can't truly understand the male psyche without understanding what we call the *Fantasy Woman syndrome*. Most men have an exact mental picture of what their ideal woman will look like. She may be tall and blonde, petite and dark, slim, or voluptuous. Some men are turned on by breasts, some men notice only legs, others are attracted to curvaceous hips, tiny waists, or prominent behinds. If you happen to be in the right place at the right time and fit the right fantasy for the right man, you don't have to do another thing. He will do all the pursuing and will become instantly infatuated with you. Suddenly people are murmuring, "Love at first sight," or "Their eyes met across a crowded room," or "He was drawn to her as if by a magnetic force."

This really does happen. Neal, a firefighter, is a perfect example of this syndrome. He was forty-three, never married, and in a five-year relationship with Libby, who he refused to marry. Libby was a hard-working, widowed mother who did all she could to keep her three kids clothed, fed, and educated. She and Neal did not live together, but they were a steady item; he was a father figure in the children's lives. He was generous with Libby and the kids, but he insisted that marriage and responsibility were not for him. Even though she wanted marriage, Libby put up with this arrangement because she loved Neal and because she was realistic enough to know if she gave him up, she would have a hard time starting over with someone else. Between working, studying for a college degree, and caring for her children, Libby didn't have the time, energy, or money to look for someone new.

One day things were slow at the fire station, and Neal and a couple of guys were standing at the door when they noticed a lovely young blonde woman riding a bicycle down the street toward them. They watched her casually until she suddenly fell off her bicycle right in front of them. Neal was the first one to arrive at her side, and he discovered she had fainted. He took one look at her and, as though lightening had struck, he was smitten. When Tina opened her big blue eyes and smiled wanly at him through pale lips, his heart did flip-flops. It turned out she was a starving artist, and she had fainted from hunger. Neal took her into his home, fed her, cared for her, waited on her, and three months later, married her. A man who thought he didn't want marriage and responsibility fell instantly in love with this stranger and couldn't do enough for her. Even though she had a three-year-old child from a previous marriage, he was ready and willing to marry her.

Why? Because she fit his fantasy. His mother, sister, and Libby were dark, but all his adult life, Neal had envisioned a fragile, pale-skinned, blue-eyed blonde as his ideal woman. When he met Tina, his fantasy came true—she didn't have to do or say a thing to be loved by him. All she had to do was accept his love and be there for him.

One of our friends saw this phenomenon take place right before her eyes, and she is still marveling over it. Iris brought her assistant, Dora, to a high-level business conference. Iris was friendly with the president of the company, Gordon, and they were standing in the reception room chatting when suddenly Gordon spotted Dora across the room. Immediately, his body language changed and his manner grew visibly distracted. He could not tear his gaze away from Dora.

"It was like an electrical charge," marveled Iris. "I could actually see and feel it!" Gordon was drawn by some invisible force across the room toward Dora.

She was a little overwhelmed but also very flattered, and they immediately became inseparable.

Even the Venus formula can't help you be someone's fantasy woman; that's in the hands of the fates. Luckily, though, while most men do have definite preferences in female beauty, they are not so rigidly defined as those of Neal and Gordon. And although physical beauty is what initially draws a man, your inner beauty is what keeps him.

Men need tenderness, sex, admiration, love, respect, comfort, nurturing, understanding, friendship, and acceptance. If they find those basics in you, they will love, nurture, protect, need, support, and adore you. In the long run, men are generally more emotionally needy than women, and when they do fall in love, they fall harder and love deeper than women. They may not always know it, and they may not always show it, but a woman who has landed her man can be sure of it.

5
Don't Waste Your Time on Dead-End Men

You're reading this book because you want to get remarried; you want to find someone with whom to spend the rest of your life. To achieve this goal you must be single-minded in your purpose and not allow yourself to be sidetracked. You must be able to determine which men are worth your time and effort. Does this mean you should date only men who you could possibly foresee marrying? Of course not. If you're just beginning to enter the dating scene after many years of marriage, you should take it slowly, let your friends set you up with someone they know and trust, and just get comfortable with your dating skills. Some women think it's fun; others are uncomfortable. In any case, don't think about finding a new husband until you have tried the single life for at least a few months.

We all have dry periods when we would gladly go

out to dinner with Godzilla just for the opportunity to get dressed up and spend a few hours in the company of a man. Most of the time it is evident after the first hour that the guy isn't Mr. Right, but sometimes a friendly face and nice conversation is a welcome alternative to sitting at home watching TV.

But once you become serious about finding another mate, don't waste your time and emotional energy on men who are dead-end dates. Rather than spend the evening with some guy you know you'll never want to date again, wouldn't you be better off doing things you otherwise wouldn't have time for, such as taking tennis, golf, bridge, or piano lessons; catching up on past-due letters; taking an aerobics class; organizing your files; entertaining friends; working for your favorite charity; going to singles functions; or doing anything that is productive and enhances your life?

FOUR TYPES WORTH GETTING TO KNOW

There are four types of men who are worth your time and energy—marriage material, the life enhancer, the toy, and the platonic friend. If you learn to recognize them, you will save yourself a lot of wasted hours.

Marriage Material

The first and most important category is the man who has the potential for a permanent relationship— a man who is *Marriage Material*. This is a man you want to marry, for whatever reasons. They may be the wrong reasons, but that is up to you to decide.

A divorced woman we know was very anxious to

get remarried because she felt she couldn't continue in her social circles without a husband. Romance and love were not her primary considerations, and within a year of her divorce, she was remarried to a man she respected and admired but didn't love. She says she is very happy and has no regrets. Her first marriage was passionate and romantic—in the beginning. It gradually turned into a disaster. She reevaluated what she wanted from marriage—an important step for anyone who wants to remarry—and decided that what she really needed was a companion with whom she could be comfortable and who shared her enjoyment in socializing and related activities. Her husband is happy and fulfilled because she uses the Venus formula to keep him happy, even after seven years of marriage. She may have married him for what some may consider the wrong reasons, but they are both getting what they want from the relationship, which is more than many couples who married for the traditional reasons can say.

Our friend Allyson, on the other hand, also married for the wrong reasons, but wasn't as lucky. She is a well-paid professional woman and prides herself on being totally independent. One of her main reasons for marrying her new mate was that he allowed her to maintain her independence. To her this means separate bank accounts, no mixing of funds, separate vacations, and many separate friends. Her husband was delighted to go along with this arrangement; he had been married twice to overly dependent women who had smothered him during marriage and subdivided his bank account when they divorced. However, after several years of marriage, Allyson realized that separateness and independence were not a good foundation for a relationship. The very qualities that had attracted her to her husband began to make her feel isolated and emotionally distanced from him. They are in the process of divorcing now.

The ideal reasons for marriage can range from love, friendship, sexual attraction, common interests, mutual compatibility—whatever you feel is right. The old cliche "different strokes for different folks" is true, and what is marriage material for one woman may not be for another.

The Life Enhancer

The possibility of marriage isn't the only criterion to use when deciding if you want to spend time with a man. The second type of man, *The Life Enhancer*, can also be a worthwhile addition to your social schedule. He may not be the person with whom you want to spend the rest of your life, but if he can offer you the opportunity to meet interesting people, take you to fabulous places, or teach you something fascinating, then he can be a terrific friend.

An acquaintance of ours has been dating a man for two years. She knows that the chances of their relationship developing into anything permanent is unlikely. He is in his forties, has never been married, and lives with his mother—not a very likely candidate for marriage. But he is deeply involved in politics, a subject with which she has had a lifelong fascination. He takes her to wonderful political events and has introduced her to the hierarchy of his party. She is his official hostess when he entertains his colleagues, and she has an inside line to all the political gossip and strategies she has always found so exciting. She also has the opportunity to meet all the other single men in the political arena on a very personal yet nonthreatening basis—as an insider.

Vera, another woman we know, has also been going with a man with whom she knows there will not be any wedding bells. He has been separated from his wife (with whom his wealth is very much intertwined) for ten years. They don't live together and they go their separate ways, but they are not likely to get divorced because of the financial considerations and because they are Catholic. But this man offers Vera something that would otherwise be very difficult for her to obtain: he is very wealthy and socially prominent. Vera, a music teacher, had a disastrous, short-lived marriage to a lazy freeloader, and now she wants the kind of lifestyle that requires a lot of money. She knows that no matter how hard she works at her chosen profession (which she loves) she won't be able to earn the kind of money she needs to live the way she *wants* to live. She is not ready or willing to settle for money without love at this point in her life, but her wealthy friend has been worth her time in several ways. He has taken her to some wonderful restaurants, concerts, and parties that she normally would not have had the opportunity to attend, she has the chance to socialize with a circle of people through which she might meet the type of man she wants to marry, and she has even acquired as new piano students the children of some of the people she has met.

The Toy

A third type of man who may be worth your while is *The Toy*. He is someone with whom you have great, uncomplicated, exciting sex. Oh, don't fall off your chair in horror. There is nothing wrong with a mature, emotionally stable woman enjoying a man for purely physical reasons. Of course, you shouldn't get involved on that level if you tend to let your emotions get the best of you and if you can't separate sex from love in your mind.

Needless to say, we are not advocating promiscuity—no one would even consider indiscriminate sex in this day and age with the threat of AIDS increasing every day. But if you are going with a man who is obviously not your dream man in most respects, but the sex is fabulous and you enjoy his company, it's not so terrible to hang in there and enjoy the good part until you feel ready to move on.

Consider Lisa and Joe. They had both just been divorced after long marriages when they met. Neither was ready to get into the dating scene, and although they didn't have much in common, they enjoyed each other's company and were comfortable together. One thing led to another, though, and they discovered that the one thing they did have in common was sexual chemistry. So even though both of them knew they weren't suited for each other for the long haul, they had a satisfying sexual relationship for several months until their emotional scars from their divorces began to heal and they were ready to look for the real thing.

If you're thinking, "what a dishonest, rotten way to use a man!", forget it: he is enjoying it, too. What if he falls in love with you? As long as you haven't been dishonest and made promises that you never planned to keep, don't feel guilty.

The Platonic Friend

The fourth type of man you shouldn't overlook is *The Platonic Friend*. This is someone you really enjoy as a person. He can be gay, he can be your ex-brother-in-law, he can be someone with whom you really have fun and are relaxed and comfortable. There can be romance involved, but more often than not, these relationships are strictly platonic. This type of relationship can be wonderfully satisfying, and these men often remain lifelong friends even after you have found Mr. Right.

A business associate of ours, Suzanne, has had this type of relationship for many years. She met John on a blind date, and they both knew after the first evening that it wasn't going to be a major romance. The chemistry wasn't there, they had totally different lifestyles, and their goals in life were miles apart. But for some crazy reason, they really enjoyed being with each other. Their offbeat senses of humor meshed, and they both loved to gossip, shop, and pig out on junk food. They have been friends for more than ten years. She is now married, and he is involved in a serious romance, but they still like to get together and gossip over chili burgers and french fries.

Many women have this type of friendship with gay men. Rita is now happily married, but she has a gay friend, Ron, with whom she has had a relationship through several romances. She still considers him one of her dearest friends. When she first met Ron at a friend's party, she didn't know he was gay, and she was attracted to him immediately. They began talking over dinner and continued talking until 3:00 A.M. During their conversation he told her he was gay, but they had so much in common and were having so much fun that it hardly mattered. They started seeing each other at least once a week and have been doing it ever since. They still go to the ballet, which they both love, to museums, and to antique shows— none of which her husband is particularly interested in. Ron is often a guest at their home for dinner, and when her husband is away on business, he escorts her to events and parties. She considers him as close as any girlfriend.

You can practice the Venus formula on all the men in your life. The degree to which you practice it will naturally be less intense with men who aren't marriage material, but dating men from whom you don't want a commitment is a wonderful way to develop those characteristics that will make you irresistible to the man you do want forever.

Remember, you don't have to worry about feeling guilty about "using" these men as a dress rehearsal for the real thing. They will be getting the benefit of having a woman make them feel really special. After all, you don't have to be in love with a person to want to make them feel important. That is a gift we should give to everyone we like well enough to spend any time with.

Hopefully, everyone reading this book is smart enough to know that if marriage is your goal, you shouldn't waste your time going out with men who are already married to someone else. These married Romeos very rarely leave their wives for their playmates, so you will more than likely find yourself on the short end of a rotten situation, no matter how much charm you exude.

KEEP AN OPEN MIND

Unfortunately, too many of the men you wind up spending time with probably don't fall into any of the four categories we describe.

How many times have you spent an evening with a man and when it's over wondered why on earth you even bothered?

How often have you accepted a boring date with a man you knew you would never see again and felt like kicking yourself because you wasted an evening you could have spent far more productively?

How often do you accept a date with someone you really couldn't care less about just to be "going out" or just so you won't be alone on Saturday night?

We're all guilty of these subterfuges. But don't forget your goal. Keep your options open. Wouldn't you be better off if you used those hours for yourself? To improve your mind, enhance your career, polish your image—even do your nails? So when the right man comes along, you will be ready.

6
Surviving the First Date

That divine man you met on the tennis court last week actually called and asked you out for Friday night. Of course, you're thrilled; the minute you heard his voice on the phone, you became enthusiastic, upbeat, amusing, and delighted to accompany him to hear the flutist Rampel, who is playing with the Symphony (you don't have the slightest idea who Rampel is, but of course, you will research him thoroughly and listen to one of his recordings before your date).

Your escort, Keith, suggests supper after the concert, and of course, you're agreeable to that, too—yes, it is too rushed to eat before; let's have a bite later and relax. So what if you have to cram down a turkey sandwich while you're putting on your makeup because you didn't have time to eat lunch on the big day?

Keith has said 7:30, and you're ready right on the minute. We guarantee he'll be on time—most men are maddeningly punctual.

Greet him with enthusiasm and a warm handshake. Look him directly in the eye and smile radiantly. Stash your kids, the dog, and your babysitter in another room at least for the first few moments of contact. You want him to concentrate solely on you and the impact you make on him. Those first thirty seconds will imprint an indelible impression of you on his mind, so plan them carefully.

You, of course, have researched Keith through the mutual friends who introduced you. You know he has two little girls, that he adores them, and that he spends every spare minute with them. In that case, see to it that your little angels are washed, combed, and powdered. Bribe them to be adorable and sweet for five minutes while you casually parade them out to meet Keith on your way to tucking the darlings in bed. Keith immediately feels warm and domestic toward you, and you conjure up all those wonderful mother images in him. "Look at those wonderful children and how sweet she is with them," is running through his mind. Never mind that you promised the kids orange fizz, pizza, and popcorn in exchange for their cooperation. It will work, and Keith will already be thinking warmly of you. Even if you don't have children, at least let Keith know early in the evening that you just love children, especially little girls.

Our friend Judy once had her sister bring over her own children in a similar situation. Judy mentioned to her date that she adored taking care of her niece and nephew as often as possible and fussed over them maternally while her date watched approvingly. He even showed them how to make an animal out of a balloon. They were duly impressed, he felt a warm glow, and after Judy and he left arm-in-arm for their big evening (supposedly leaving the kids in the care of the eldest, who was old enough to babysit), Judy's sister emerged from hiding in the bedroom and took the kids home. Judy is now stepmother to his three kids.

On the other hand, if your prior research has found that he has no children, or that his kids are grown and out of the house, or that he's skittish on the subject of family, ask the kids to stay in their rooms until after you have left, or better yet, have them sleep at a friend's house for the night.

By the way, pets fall into the same category as children. If you don't know his feelings toward animals, keep yours locked up until you find out. Carol learned this lesson the hard way. She had been trying for months to land a date with Sid. He finally invited her to a black tie charity affair, and he arrived looking splendid in his tuxedo. Carol and her two white Persian cats greeted him at the door. He had barely gotten into the house when the cats befriended him, wrapped themselves around his legs, and proceeded to shed white fur all over his new tuxedo. Sid tried to be a good sport about it, but he was visibly unnerved.

Carol apologized profusely and ran for the lint brush. Then Sid started to sneeze and his eyes began watering. Naturally, Carol didn't know he was violently allergic to cats, but the damage was done. She was nervous and agitated and he was embarrassed and uncomfortable. It was definitely not the charming, relaxed prelude to a terrific evening that she had anticipated. She never knew whether it was the cats or just the wrong vibes, but he never called her for a second date.

So remember, that first impression is very important.

"WHAT AM I GOING TO WEAR?"

Now you've handled the problem of the kids and pets, and you and Keith are on your way to the concert. Of course, you have dressed to show off your best points: if you've got good legs, wear a dress to show them off; if your bust is a selling point, suggest your curves. But don't be *too* sexy or blatant. On a first date, it's hard to gauge what attracts a man physically, so moderate and discreet is usually best.

Mickie was once fixed up with a man who, Mickie was told, was a refined intellectual of European background. He was dignified, a little formal, and interested in art, culture, and world affairs. He telephoned Mickie for a date and suggested an elegant French restaurant. Knowing all this background, she purposely dressed down, using her most refined look. She wore a burgundy silk dress with a high neck and long sleeves, one strand of pearls, small earrings, and high-heeled pumps. She looked very elegant, but not particularly sexy. He wore, as she had imagined he would, a three-piece suit.

So she had figured him out correctly, right? Wrong! During the evening he pointed out several women at the restaurant and later at a cocktail lounge who he thought were attractive. Mickie thought that they looked like hookers, but of course, she just nodded in agreement.

Right then she realized that he was one of those men who is a paradox. They themselves are straight-laced, prim, and proper, but they like their women spicy and sexy—and flaunting it. How should she have known? By researching him more thoroughly. The friend who fixed them up knew his former wife and later told Mickie she was a blonde bombshell, sort of a European Charo. So even though they had a

lot in common intellectually and he told the friend
that Mickie was one of the brightest and best-in-
formed women he had ever met, he never called her
again. He told their friend she didn't turn him on—he
just didn't feel that sexual spark. He is now going
steady with a woman who flaunts everything she has
and makes no secret of her 36D bosom.

You can't win them all, of course, but the more
research you do on a man, the better you will be able
to seem like his fantasy woman, and that's half the
battle. In the end, if the man enjoys your company,
he'll be back for more.

Don't push too hard; let him set the pace. It's better
if he plans the evening and, of course, you're going to
love that darling little bistro he discovered last week.
He has such instinctively good taste! The table he
selects will be just perfect. The temperature in the
restaurant will be ideal (even if you're seated under
the air conditioning vent), and you won't bore him
with the reasons you can't eat garlic, onions, or rad-
ishes.

Believe it or not, some men still prefer a woman to
make her selection from the menu, inform her escort,
and allow *him* to tell the waiter. This may sound
silly and old-fashioned but it happens, so keep it in
mind.

"SHOULD I OFFER TO PAY MY SHARE ON THE FIRST DATE?"

Should you offer to pay your share on this first date?
Our considered opinion is no, especially if *he* asked
you out. But there seems to be an age gap that has a
definite bearing on who pays. If you and your date are
under thirty, both still in school, or both just starting

out in careers, and your salaries are roughly equal, then it's sometimes acceptable to share the check. Many younger men don't feel the least bit threatened or "unmanly" if their date offers to pay. In fact, they may be relieved. However, if you do offer and he refuses, don't make an issue of it. Just smile your thanks and keep your money—you can make it up another time.

If a man is over thirty-five, and definitely if he is over forty, and well-established in his work, just assume he is going to pay. He wants to pay; it makes him feel important. You expect to be taken care of and treated like a lady, and he expects to pay.

It is true that money can be power, so it's understandable why some feminists (as well as male writers such as Warren Farrell in *Why Men Are the Way They Are*) insist that if a man pays for dinner, he is, in effect, buying your company and therefore thinks he has a right to expect "repayment" later. The logic here is that if you establish your equality right at the beginning, he will appreciate your independence.

To this line of reasoning we say, baloney. First of all, no man is buying anything except two dinners. He is courting you—period. Your only obligation is to be as pleasant a companion as possible. You don't owe him another thing. Remember, you're someone very special. He's lucky you accepted this date with him. It should thrill him to wine and dine someone as charming as you.

The overwhelming majority of men we asked about this issue said they would be insulted if the woman offered to pay. And far from applauding her independence, they said they would be put off and would consider her unfeminine. They also said that if a woman insists on paying her share, she is signaling that she is not interested in him sexually and that she wants only a platonic relationship.

There is a subtle, sexual mating dance that goes on between the sexes, and part of a man's ego is wrapped up in his wallet. So if you are interested in this man as a potentially serious relationship, leave your credit card at home and let him take charge of the check. If you are *not* interested in him as a possible future mate or date, then accept the risk of offending him and pay your own way.

If, on the other hand, *you* have asked the man out specifically to lunch, dinner, or the theatre, then the rules change for that occasion. If you did the inviting and he accepted on that basis, don't wait for him to reach for the check. Prearrange payment with the maitre d', or purchase the tickets in advance. A man will really appreciate that show of class. Even then, most men will want to pay for *some* part of the evening, and you should let him buy drinks before dinner or a snack after the theatre if he offers. Most men feel slightly off balance and guilty if they let a woman pay for the whole evening.

After you have dated a while, you can repay your man's generosity by inviting him for a home-cooked meal, asking him to escort you to a glamorous party, or just happening to have a pair of tickets to a sporting event, movie, or theatre. Later on, when you are an established twosome, you can make any kind of financial arrangement that's mutually agreeable.

But this is your first date. You don't want to do or say anything to offend or embarrass him. Unless he point blank asks for your share, keep your wallet closed, put a smile on your face, and let him handle the bill.

SAYING GOODNIGHT:
WHAT DOES HE EXPECT?

Saying goodnight on a first date can be awkward. Our advice is to make it short and sweet. Don't go to his place, and don't invite him in to yours for a nightcap. Say goodnight in the lobby or at your door. Have your keys out, and as you're unlocking the door, turn to him, put out your hand, and in your most charming, adorable, intimate manner, take his hand in both of yours, smile warmly, and tell him what a wonderful evening it was and how much you enjoyed his company. And then disappear—gracefully and quickly.

If he liked you at all, he will be back for more because he will be intrigued. You've left him a little off-balance. You seemed to genuinely like him, but you didn't wait around for the "I'll call you" or let any awkward moments set in. You stayed in control and didn't seem one bit anxious to know when or if there would be another date. That usually spurs a man on to the chase. All of us at one time or another have let an evening linger on too long; what started out as enchanting ends up as mundane. Pacing and timing are important. Always leave him wanting a little more.

And that leads us to sex. If this is a man you might want on a permanent basis, *never*, *never*, no matter how magic the night may seem, no matter how full the moon or how sweet the Jasmine scented air, *never* go to bed with a man on the first date. A few playful kisses perhaps, but not even any heavy necking. This is an absolute.

Of course, there is an exception to every rule. We all know couples who say they fell into bed after the first hour together, didn't come up for air for three days, and have been happily married for twenty years. But they are definitely the exception, and you want the best odds. Most women admit that when they've succumbed to passion too soon, they've regretted it.

If you do go to bed with him on the first date and, as often happens the first time, things are less than perfect, you can be sure he won't be back. Why should he? He hardly knows you. There has been no buildup of intimacy, and he's probably disappointed or embarrassed. So why should he bother? Don't take the chance of losing him that way—he is far more likely to find you intriguing if you're not that easy. And, as you should know, the anticipation makes the real thing even more exciting.

He may protest, but deep down men like the thrill of the chase. Sex has been so available during the last few years that it's hardly a great commodity to offer anymore. *You* are what's going to intrigue a man, so hold off until your relationship has established a steady pattern and some emotional intimacy. Don't be rushed.

FIRST DATE DOs AND DON'Ts

- *Don't* get into heavy conversations—the nasty divorce, rotten love affair, miserable life, lousy shrink, and so forth.

- *Don't* talk about your ex-husband except in the most casual way, and don't say anything derogatory or get into details.

- *Don't* smoke unless he does.

- *Don't* come on too strong about anything.

- *Don't* ask for favors, such as replacing a light bulb or taking home the sitter.

- *Don't* tell anecdotes about people he doesn't know, and don't gossip maliciously.

- *Don't* drink too much.

- *Don't* seem strained and anxious.

- *Don't* laugh or talk too loudly.

- *Don't* talk about sex except in a light way—don't get into intimate details.

- *Don't* tell your entire life story.

- *Do* listen to *his* entire life story.

- *Do* be on time—most men hate to wait.

- *Do* smile and greet him warmly.

- *Do* be charming and put him at ease.

- *Do* show him you like him and express appreciation.

- *Do* find an outstanding feature or virtue about him and compliment him on it.

- *Do* memorize and practice the Venus formula and you'll be on your way to that second date.

7
Mixed Signals, Hidden Meanings, and Mistaken Illusions

The biggest complaint we hear from women is that no matter how many times they have been married or for how long, they just don't understand men (men claim they don't understand women, either, but that's another book). When women complain they don't understand men, they mean they don't understand men's actions toward them. They may have understood their husband, but the attitudes of society, as well as the new men they are meeting really puzzle them. How many hours have women spent on Monday morning phone calls with their best friends, wondering, "Why didn't he call me like he promised?" "We seemed to have such a fabulous evening together, why haven't I heard from him again?" "He was so turned on to me and said I was wonderful, so where is he?" "He said he was looking for a relationship, and we seemed so right for each other, so what's the problem?" And on and on.

After talking to many men, doing a great deal of research, and having been guinea pigs ourselves, we've come to the simple conclusion that men and women think differently and speak a different language. As we've already discussed in Chapter 3, "Understanding the Male Mystique," men usually aren't as in touch with their feelings as women are, so they tend not to be as straightforward in the mating game. This is not because they are rotten, unfeeling bastards; it's because they most likely are confused about their feelings, ambivalent about their needs, and afraid of their emotions. This sometimes causes erratic and unexplainable behavior, which drives women crazy.

Marilyn and Jon were on their second date and were getting along beautifully. They were talking about their lives and the conversation turned to relationships. Jon said he was tired of the dating scene and was looking for a committed relationship. Marilyn interpreted this statement to mean that he was considering her for this blissful state. Since that was what Marilyn wanted also, and since she found Jon the most attractive, interesting man who had come her way in a long time, she was already fantasizing their future together.

That night they made love. Emotionally it was very satisfying—for Marilyn. Physically they still had a lot to learn about each other's sexual needs and responses, but to Marilyn that was a small concern. She knew true sexual compatibility doesn't happen in one night, that it takes time to build up the trust, openness, and understanding for true sexual ecstasy.

Marilyn, in other words, was already projecting a future with Jon. After all, Jon had told her he wanted a committed relationship. He could hardly keep his hands or eyes off her all evening. During lovemaking he told her how wonderful she was, how soft and gentle and warm. He seemed so caring, so tuned in to her. She even let him stay the night, reveling in his body's warmth and mentally planning all sorts of wonderful future activities for them—her vacation, his vacation, next weekend, Thanksgiving.

In the morning, Jon seemed a little distant and anxious to leave. It was Sunday, and Marilyn had thought that they would have a leisurely breakfast together, then maybe drive to the beach or go to a museum—then spend another evening making love. Instead, Jon said he had a golf game scheduled at ten o'clock and, after a quick cup of coffee and a shower, he was ready to leave. Marilyn had a sinking feeling in the pit of her stomach. This wasn't at all the romantic idyll she had envisioned. Jon suddenly seemed like a stranger, and Marilyn didn't know what to do or say. Jon kissed her gently at the door, told her, "It was just great, I'll call you," and was gone. Marilyn collapsed on the bed sobbing. She never heard from Jon again. And all her sympathetic girlfriends told her what a bastard he was—just like most men. He had fed her a line and used her.

Marilyn made several mistakes with Jon. First, she went to bed with him on only the second date, much too soon for any emotional bond to be established between them. Second, she heard only what she wanted to hear in Jon's words and interpreted them through her own needs and hopes. Jon didn't say he wanted a relationship with *her*, and maybe he really didn't want a committed relationship with anyone. It was just an idea he was toying with, and he expressed it to Marilyn after a few drinks in a vulnerable moment. When he made love to her, he said loving things that many men say in the heat of passion. "You're wonderful," "I can't get enough of you," "You excite me," "Your body feels so terrific."

Marilyn didn't recognize the limits of sweet talk. She hadn't learned not to put stock in promises made during lovemaking. Jon wasn't really a bastard. His agenda was just different from Marilyn's. He thought she was nice and he enjoyed the sex, but bells didn't go off for him. He felt no emotional compulsion to hurry back to Marilyn. The chances are very strong that if Marilyn hadn't gone to bed with him, he still would never have called her again. But Marilyn would have felt a lot better about herself. Jon probably had no idea that Marilyn had much deeper feelings about this encounter than he did and would be genuinely surprised to know he had hurt her.

LOVE VS. LUST: HOW TO TELL THE DIFFERENCE

Most of us have had at least one unhappy experience like Marilyn's. How can we avoid falling into the fantasy trap the next time? By understanding that what a man says is not always what he means. By listening closely to the way he says intimate things, and by getting to know him well enough to know whether his actions match his words. By recognizing that sex is different for men than it is for most women; most men can separate sex from love or even from strong emotion and forget about it the next day. And by realizing that *sex talk* is not *love talk*. Sex talk is spoken in the heat of passion and should be promptly forgotten when that passion is spent. Love talk takes place anywhere—after sex, when the words are spoken from the heart, not the hormones; over the phone; over a cup of morning coffee; in a quiet, cozy moment.

Many men are not good at talking, so the old adage "actions speak louder than words" has a great deal of validity. If a man is genuinely interested in you, he will let you know it by wanting to see you again. He will be concerned with your welfare. He will miss you. He will want to be with you on a regular basis, and he will call you often. You won't have to set up a lonely vigil by the phone wondering if he will call. He will *want* to call, if only to touch base with you. Only after he gives you these signals should you begin to take his interest seriously. And even then, you still can't be too careful.

Be wary of the man who employs what we call the rush technique, which usually lasts about six weeks. He does all the right things—in fact, he does almost too many of the right things. He'll overwhelm you with attention, affection, calls, gifts, flowers. He'll make you feel adored, loved, queenly. And just about the time you're ready to succumb to his charms and return his attention with your genuine love, he disappears, leaving you hurt, bewildered, angry, and emotionally devastated. Was he captured by a terrorist? Did his car go over a cliff? Is he in the hospital with a brain tumor? Did you do something to chase him away? *What happened?*

Nothing much happened. These men are just living out their fantasies. They are usually emotionally shallow and not easily capable of mature, long-lasting love. No matter how successful they are in their careers, emotionally they are adolescent boys chasing the prom queen. It's fun for a while, but pretty soon the prom queen is no longer a fantasy—she turns out to be a real flesh and blood girl—and so the game is no longer exciting. That's when Mr. Wonderful gets restless and goes off looking, once again, for a new fantasy woman.

Our friend Stacy is a classic victim of the rush technique. In her job as a magazine editor, she attends many business dinners and cocktail parties. Stacy is a glamorous blonde and men have always been attracted to her, but she was always very choosy and picked her men carefully. Because she had been married twice and dated so many men, she assumed that she understood them pretty well. At one party, she met Stewart, a big teddy bear of a man, very charming and self-assured. He was immediately captivated by Stacy and let her know it. They left the party and went to a small, intimate cocktail lounge and talked and talked. He was so interested in her, so obviously smitten with her, that Stacy couldn't help but respond. After all, Stewart was attractive, interesting, worldly, successful, and obviously taken with her—what woman wouldn't be flattered? From that night on they were rarely apart. Stewart sent her flowers almost daily. He took her on shopping sprees. On a weekend out of town he surprised her with a beautiful gold necklace. He treated her like a queen. Nothing was too good for her. No request was refused. And the lovemaking! Stacy later said that his prowess in bed had spoiled her for all other men. She was falling hard.

About three weeks into their relationship, Stewart had to go to San Francisco for a week, and they decided that Stacy would meet him there for a "honeymoon" weekend. He called her twice a day from San Francisco and told her how excited he was about the upcoming weekend. Everything was planned down to the last detail. Stacy was flown first class. A limousine was waiting for her at the airport. In the limo was a box from Saks with a magnificent night-gown inside and a note, "Waiting for you, my love. Stewart."

He was waiting for her in a beautiful suite in the best hotel in San Francisco. Also waiting for her were two dozen roses and a bottle of Dom Perignon champagne. It was all so romantic and overwhelming that Stacy just collapsed in his arms. By the time the weekend was over, Stacy was hopelessly in love. Why shouldn't she be? Wouldn't you?

A couple of weeks or so after their return home, Stacy detected a slight cooling off. She couldn't pin it down but somehow the affair wasn't progressing as she thought it would. By now they should have developed a comfortable intimacy, but she felt on edge. He was calling less often and making excuses not to see her. Stacy felt panicked. She knew she was losing him, but she didn't know why. Finally, she asked him what was wrong, and he came up with the old excuse that "maybe he needed more space." He was feeling hemmed-in, and so on, and so forth. Stacy was thoroughly bewildered. She hadn't asked him to chase her—it was his idea—and now that he had made her fall in love with him, he was backing off. It wasn't fair. She didn't confront him with her dilemma because she was afraid of losing him, but, of course, she lost him anyway. As fast as it started, the affair was over, leaving Stacy devastated. She cried for weeks and swore she'd never trust another man again.

This is why our motto is: if it seems like too much, too soon—it probably is! Only time will tell whether a man is serious and in for the long haul, or whether he's just playing little-boy fantasy games with you. If the relationship is still going strong after six or eight weeks and you have found you can rely on his consistency, if your relationship has reached a level that's comfortable and relaxed for you, *then* you can let down your emotional guard. Any sooner than that, keep up the warning flags.

This doesn't mean that you can't enjoy a new man's attentions and return them with your own. But until you're very sure of his intentions and his emotional maturity, look at the affair as a game. Flirt and revel in his attentions, but keep your deepest emotions in check so that you won't be hurt if one day he suddenly pulls back and disappears. You don't ever want to lose control of the relationship because once you do, it's very difficult to regain. And once you lose control of yourself, your self-esteem will plunge to the depths. Men like Stewart drive women crazy, but unless you learn to recognize them and deal with them, you will be very vulnerable to every one you meet.

"BUT HE SAID HE'D CALL"

Another mixed message men send is to get very enthused on a date, make future plans with you, and never follow through.

Mary was on a second date with Mark. She really liked him, and they seemed to have much in common. During dinner she mentioned the Monterey Jazz Festival; Mark said he attended every year, and this year they would have to go together. Later on, Mark commented on a movie he wanted to see. Mary wanted to see it, too, and Mark said, "Great. I'll take you." Toward the end of the evening, Mark, an architect, said, "Next time we go out, I'd like you to see that building I told you about." By this time, Mary was envisioning many future dates with Mark, and she was overflowing with anticipation. Imagine her disappointment when Mark never called again. What

Mary didn't know was that Mark was just a very enthusiastic person full of wonderful ideas that always seemed terrific to him at the moment, but lost their shine later on. He probably didn't even remember what he said in the exhilaration of the moment. But how was Mary to know that?

SEX: WHEN IS IT RIGHT?

Another danger sign is when a man is overly demanding about sex in his timetable, not yours. Say you've had a few dates with a man you like but would rather get to know better before having sex; he refuses to hold the line at kissing and keeps trying for more, until you feel uncomfortable at having to repeatedly push him away. This man is telling you a lot about himself. He's telling you he's selfish, insensitive, impatient, demanding, and doesn't respect you as a person in your own right.

Unfortunately, we've all endured situations like this. These men are usually charming and seem very desirable and if we keep saying no, we feel childish and silly. So very often we give in, afraid of losing him. But because we really weren't emotionally ready for sex with this man, we wind up feeling awful afterward. And chances are, the man won't come back anyway. Or if he does, it wasn't because of the sex, it was because he liked you, but now you'll never know which was which. When a sexual relationship starts too soon, it usually takes precedence in the man's mind and he will feel less inclined to make the effort required to get to know *you* any more deeply.

Psychologists who have studied this phenomenon report that a relationship usually stays emotionally where it was when sex entered it. If you have a shallow, casual relationship and have started a sexual union, later, when you want the relationship to mature and deepen, you're going to have a hard time changing it. If you're really serious about your man, wait until you feel you're ready, no matter how hard he pushes. If he's the right man, he'll respect your commitment to yourself, and even though he might not understand it, he'll be patient. If he gets huffy and drops you, then he was the wrong man anyway. Remember, you're looking for a lifetime commitment, not a casual affair.

You must strike a very delicate balance between being cold and standoffish and being warm and sexy but not ready to go all the way. Many men will think you're being silly and will say you're acting like a teenager. Even *you* may feel slightly ridiculous holding off. After all, you lost your virginity long ago. You both know you were previously married and what's the big deal anyway?

The big deal is that if you don't want to sleep with him, you don't have to. Our best advice is to let him know plainly, sweetly, and firmly what your moral code is, and stick to it without apology or long justifications. But at the same time, be warm and affectionate. Kiss and embrace him, but keep your clothes on, buttons buttoned, zippers zipped (that goes for him too). Never let things get out of hand. You will have to maintain the control; don't expect him to. It's definitely a mixed signal if you let your physical passions overwhelm you one night, but then realize you aren't psychologically ready and suddenly pull back. You will lose a man with behavior like that.

Just remember who you are and what you want from this man. If you stick to your code with explanations such as "I just don't feel ready yet," "You're so attractive, but sex is *very* special to me," "I know you think I'm silly, but that's just the way I was brought up," "I love sex, but only with a man I'm in love with," and so on, he'll come back for more.

WHAT YOU SEE IS WHAT YOU'RE GOING TO GET

The more men you date, the more you'll find that men show their true nature in their dating habits. You can find out about their manners, morals, temperament, regard for others, and attitudes toward money, sex, children, women, and humanity in general. If a man isn't polite, dependable, concerned, and interested in you on the first date—when he supposedly wants to impress you—what will he be like later, after the relationship is more established and he *really* lets his guard down?

Mickie once had a blind date with a man who was a customer of her friend, Reba. Reba found him very attractive herself, but he seemed to be interested in her only as a business friend. Following the theory "never let a good man get away—if he's not right for you, fix him up with a friend and wish her better luck," Reba told Don to call Mickie. He did, promptly, and sounded interesting and fun over the phone. He asked her out to dinner Saturday night and said, "Dress casually," which is usually a euphemism for "Don't expect a fancy, expensive restaurant." That was OK—for a first date. Reba had warned Mickie that he didn't like to dress up and enjoyed looking antiestablishment; he was also a gourmet cook and had formerly been a restaurant critic. Mickie figured he would probably have some favorite out-of-the-way haunts in mind, and it might be fun. He asked over the phone what kind of food she liked, she said that anything would be fine, and since he was so knowledgeable about food, she'd be delighted to have him

choose the place. He was due at 7:30, and promptly at
7:30, Don appeared. Mickie was wearing black
leather pants, a simple cream silk shirt, a wide
leather belt, and flats—her only jewelry was a pair of
big gold hoop earrings. For her, that's Saturday night
casual. Don, on the other hand, looked as if he had
just finished working in his yard. He wore baggy, ill-
fitting, blue cotton work pants, a brown nondescript
T-shirt topped with a cotton plaid lumberman's shirt
that wasn't tucked in, and tennis shoes. Everything
was wrinkled. There was a day's worth of stubble on
his face. Unless he was trying to grow a beard, he had
not bothered to shave. He looked disheveled and
certainly had made no efforts to impress the new
woman he was meeting for the first time.

After the first moments of greeting, he said, "I
didn't know you were going to dress up!" Mickie just
smiled and said lightly, "Oh, you know how women
love to play dress-up." Inside she was furious at his
obvious lack of manners and interest in her, thinking
that even if she was going out with a woman friend
on Saturday night, she wouldn't wear sloppy clothes;
there is a difference between casual and sloppy.

Don immediately told her that he had just torn
himself away from an absorbing project he was working on, that he was hungry, and that he hadn't had a
chance to make dinner plans. He said all this nicely
and with a touch of self-deprecating humor. But
where did it leave her? She felt as if she was somehow
intruding on his life. It seemed that instead of looking forward to meeting her, he was treating the evening as an afterthought. He had put no thought or
planning into the date.

There is nothing worse than starting out an evening with someone new and then having to decide
where to go. You don't know his tastes or wallet size;

he doesn't know your food idiosyncrasies. Each one is trying to be polite, but you're both distracted, wondering what place would be suitable and whether it will be crowded. Not a very auspicious way to start an evening.

They eventually landed at a pleasant bistro in the neighborhood, and Mickie proceeded to try to get to know this stranger. The more interesting the man, the easier it is to do. This man *was* interesting and had a fascinating background. During the evening, he told her he was in therapy to try to learn more about himself, his relations with women, and why both his former wives accused him of lack of intimacy. Mickie felt like telling him he didn't need all that therapy, that after two hours in his company, she could tell him exactly what was wrong. Of course, she didn't. She listened to his stories, sympathized with his problems, enthused over his projects, and told him how interesting and accomplished he was.

Well, Mickie is interesting and accomplished, too, but he never found that out because, like so many men, he never asked questions about her. He casually asked her what she does, and she told him she was working on a new book—her third. He never followed that remark up, never asked what the books were about, who published them—nothing. That might have been okay with some women (especially if Don had been incredibly wonderful in other areas), but Mickie found him to be just plain rude.

Now, we tell you this episode because it illustrates our premise—what you see is what you're going to get. This man, while very charming, witty, and bright, is also self-involved, emotionally ungiving, inconsiderate of others' feelings, unconcerned with appearances, and probably hostile to women. He might fit into one of the four categories of men you'll want to keep seeing, but he surely isn't material for a long-term relationship.

You must be able to recognize these men and not fantasize that they're going to change to fill your needs. Enjoy these men for what they are, if you can. If you're not emotionally capable of handling them, then don't get involved in the first place. You will only get hurt.

ROMANCE JUNKIES

There are other types of men to beware of. For example, the "romance junkie." He doesn't seem to have any deep emotional needs for intimacy or closeness. He is usually very attractive and highly eligible, and he makes a wonderful date. He does and says all the right things, and unless a woman is aware of this man's limitations, she will invariably be charmed by him and fantasize about her future with him. On the first date he probably will be very warm and complimentary and might make romantic overtures varying from a sweet kiss to more passionate embraces. The woman he's with will usually be so enthralled with him that she responds warmly. When he never calls her again, she is, of course, crushed and runs to her female friends with the universal questions, "Why?", "What happened?", "What did I do wrong?"

She didn't do anything wrong. He is a romance junkie and got his emotional fill from that wonderful, warm evening. He got his ego stroked. He saw his charm reflected in her eyes. He got his physical hugs and kisses. He had a delightful evening, and he doesn't need anything more from her. The next night he repeats the pattern all over again with another woman. He's usually a nice guy and will say only the most flattering things about all of his dates. He doesn't promise anything specific, and he would be genuinely shocked if he knew how often women took his attentions seriously. For him, dating is just a wonderful game, and he never tires of it no matter how old he gets.

How do you recognize this kind of man and either avoid him or enjoy the game for the momentary thrill? You can't always be sure on the first or second date (which may be all you'll get). But there are some clues to look for: if he's over thirty and has never been married, in love, or had a long, committed relationship with a woman; if he's over forty and had a very brief marriage years ago and no long commitments since; if he's very social and goes out a great deal; if he likes to travel alone. These men are perfectly content with shallow, fleeting relationships and honestly don't want or need anything deeper.

Another kind of man who is difficult to pin down is the one with "commitmentitis." This is a disease of almost epidemic proportions among available men today. These men are so afraid of commitment that they will sabotage a relationship to avoid it. However, they usually do settle down, eventually.

Also be wary of the man who has just ended a serious relationship. He might be newly divorced or just split with a long-time love, but he's usually very hurt, bitter, or wary of new entanglements. He also might bolt the minute he starts liking you too much.

"JUST LOOKING, THANKS"

Another broad category of man who emits mixed signals is the "just looking, thanks" guy who doesn't really know what he wants. He says he wants a serious relationship, and he probably even *thinks* he wants one. But deep down, he really doesn't. No woman seems quite right for him, and he goes from one to another hoping he'll find that elusive, perfect someone. He's not willing to put any time or energy into a relationship to make it work, so he keeps on shopping. He's the man at the local singles bar every Friday night or the one who invariably turns up at every singles dance and networking party. He will often run an ad in the singles column of the paper or join a computer dating service. That way he has a steady smorgasbord of available women to date. He will go out with quite a few of them and earnestly declare his intentions of finding Ms. Right. But somehow they always turn out to be Ms. Wrong for him. He won't ask you out a second or third time, either. He never really enjoys his dates because he's too busy looking for flaws. He is one of the toughest types to spot unless you know his history or have seen him at too many singles affairs. If he does date a woman for any length of time, he'll begin finding fault with her. This kind of man will drive you crazy and threaten your self-esteem because you can't please him—he doesn't want you to. If you meet a guy like this, run for your life.

DEALING WITH ELUSIVE MEN

There's nothing much you can do about any of these elusive men except practice the Venus formula and hope for the best. If you've done your research on him then you know pretty well whether he fits any of the above categories. If he does, don't blame yourself if he suddenly drops out of your life—you've done nothing wrong. It's his problem, not yours. It only becomes your problem if you *think* it's your fault or if you've allowed yourself to get emotionally hooked on him. We know that's easily done, because very often these

unobtainable men seem the most desirable of all. We
don't know a woman who hasn't had her heart broken
at least once by one of them.

Although we told you earlier not to believe what a
man says unless his actions match his words, in the
case of the foregoing men, you *should* listen to what
they say. If a man tells you he's not ready for a new
relationship yet, believe him. If he tells you he loves
his single lifestyle, believe him. If he says his last
wife took advantage of him and now he doesn't trust
women, believe him. If he says marriage is old-fashioned and he doesn't want children, believe him.

Some of these men will eventually change their
minds and marry, but only when the timing is right
for them. As the saying goes, luck and timing *are*
everything in life, so if you're not lucky enough to
meet the right man for you at the right time for *him*,
nothing will make it work.

WHAT SIGNALS DO YOU GIVE OFF?

Very often we don't see ourselves as others see us or
we don't understand that how we look, walk, talk,
act, and carry ourselves gives off a certain impression to others, especially men, and it might be the
wrong impression.

There is, for instance, the question: do women
dress for men or for each other? What is fashion,
anyhow? Most men don't notice what a woman is
wearing. They just notice a general impression of her
that registers favorably or unfavorably. If she wears a
dress that's short and tight, he might not notice the
dress, but he will notice the outline of her figure in it.
If he likes what he sees, then he likes the dress, even
though he probably couldn't even tell you what color
it is the next day. If a woman wears 3½" heels and has

knockout legs, a man will notice the legs, not the shoes. He won't know or care whether you paid $30 or $130 for them. He just knows whether or not your legs impressed him. We've all known very attractive men who wind up with pretty but incredibly tacky-looking women, and while we gossip among ourselves about her lack of taste and style, the happy couple is oblivious. He thinks she's beautiful, and she makes him feel good. He doesn't know or care whether or not her skirt is too long or too short, or too full or too flowered to suit this year's fashion dictates.

In fact, dressing too fashionably and up-to-the-minute will intimidate a lot of men. They will feel they can't keep up with you socially or financially.

Della is one such fashion plate. She has a model's slim, long-legged figure and elegant carriage. She buys all the fashion magazines and spends every dime on clothes. Her women friends think she's stunning and look forward to seeing Della's new outfits. If minis are in, she wears minis, with all the right accessories. If the long, romantic look is this year's rage, Della floats in ruffles and lace. If ethnic is hot, Della trots out her tribal look. If it's silver jewelry this season, Della could open a silver mine. Several of the men Della dated regularly told her friends they had stopped seeing her *because* of her emphasis on fashion: it signaled to them that she was a shallow person with a poor value system. One man said he enjoyed showing Della off to his friends because she always looked so stunning, but he could never imagine her all messed up after a sexual bout. Della seemed encased in cellophane; men couldn't imagine her sweating. In spite of her good figure and high-style looks, Della just didn't seem sexy.

She is actually a very warm, earthy woman and

every bit as comfortable in her birthday suit as she is in Chanel. But she was giving off the wrong signals to men. When she finally realized it, she began to play it safe until she knew the man's preference. If he was a meat-and-potatoes guy, she left the high-fashion gear in her closet and wore something smart but simple until he was comfortable with her; then, once in a while, she would wear something extravagant and watch his reaction. If he didn't notice at all, then she realized he saw the woman, not the clothes, and it probably didn't matter what she wore. If he commented negatively, she took the hint, and if he loved it, she told him how delighted she was that he noticed and appreciated her "new" image. She is now steadily dating Guy, who thinks her high-fashion look is a kick, but who admits he never would have taken her out again if she had appeared in one of her expensive get-ups on their first few dates.

Like Della, many women sabotage themselves inadvertently by giving off mixed signals. One of the most common complaints we hear from men is that many women seem hard, aggressive, and insensitive. This is probably true. Not that they *are* that way— they just *seem* that way. We can certainly understand this because life can be tough for a single woman, both professionally and socially. We've had to put up with a lot, and sometimes our patience grows thin in the dating jungle. But men back away from this kind of woman, so if you suspect you might be one of them, ask a former date or a close male friend or even a woman friend to tell you how you appear to them. Ask them to especially notice how you act around men.

Lena is an energetic, very pretty, articulate real estate saleswoman. All day long she is selling, convincing, negotiating, She is very aggressive in an extremely competitive business, and is known in her field as a hard-driving, hard-working, straight-talking professional. She is also very successful.

There is another side to Lena that very few people know. She has a retarded daughter who she is caring for in the best institution and to whom she is devoted. She also supports a crippled brother. She is a wonderful friend and is always there when someone needs her. But Lena is a proud woman and very few people, certainly not her dates, see this private, nurturing side of her. She doesn't want anyone to feel sorry for her, so she hides her vulnerable side and shows a tough, self-assured, and super-efficient stance to the world. Men interpret this to be aggressive, "ball-breaking," and arrogant. "She doesn't need me," lamented Evan. "She doesn't need anybody!" Lena has lost man after man because, in spite of being pretty and feminine-looking at first glance, men can't break through her defenses when they first get to know her. The sad thing is that she is very soft and vulnerable and yearns to have someone care for her and share her life. She's just too proud to show it.

Then, of course, there are women who dress and act sexy and then wonder why they have to fight the guy off at the end of the evening. That's not fair, ladies! And lots of men complain about it. Of all the mixed signals women give men, this "come here—don't touch" game is the one that drives them the most crazy. If you dress and act like a hooker or Hollywood bimbo, what do you expect from the poor guy? If all evening you're flirting and flaunting your 36C bosom and centerfold bottom, how can you expect him to believe that you're not looking for more than a goodnight handshake at the door? It takes very little to excite a man, and we have all had to fight off a man or two even when we haven't acted or dressed particularly sexy. So don't turn him on and then get angry at the anxious guy. He's just following your lead and his instincts. Now, you're certainly free to look and act subtly sexy—you want him to know you're a desirable woman. But moderation does it in both dress and decorum.

Among other mixed signals women give off is acting scatter-brained when you really are very intelligent. This is usually an affliction of extremely good-looking women who feel that no one is interested in their intelligence anyway. There is nothing wrong in admitting to both beauty and brains. Women who act, look, and talk like little girls won't be taken seriously by men, or anyone else.

An indecisive woman is another type who drives men up the wall. The woman who constantly says she doesn't care what movie to see or which restaurant to choose is really putting all the burden on the man. In the beginning of the relationship, this is fine and we recommend it, but as you get to know each other, it becomes annoying. Besides, it's dishonest—and the man knows it. Thinking that a man likes your constant deference is a mistake.

Rosa is one of these women. Every time she went out with Felix, she invariably left the plans up to him. She said she didn't care what movie they saw, so he picked it. She insisted she had no preference for the restaurant, so he chose. She didn't care where they went on vacation, so he planned it. At first, he enjoyed being totally in charge, but eventually it became an effort. Also, if the movie, dinner, or vacation turned out to be third-rate, Felix felt responsible and slightly guilty, as though the whole thing was his fault. Finally, one day when Rosa complained about one of his choices, he blew up, and they had a rousing fight that left Rosa in tears. She finally admitted that she *thought* he wanted to choose everything. Certainly she had opinions and ideas of her own—she had just mistakenly withheld them. When they finally straightened out the signals, they saved their relationship.

In other words, decide very carefully what image you want to project, and then work very conscientiously to see that you *do* give out those vibes. If you want to be protected and nurtured, don't come off as hard and abrasive. If you want to be respected for your intellect, don't be silly and vapid. If you don't want to be thought of as easy, then don't look or act that way. If you want to project calmness and ease, then don't act nervous and disorganized.

And don't forget the rules of fair play. If you are not interested in a man, don't lead him on. Don't play the same devastating emotional games that men sometimes play on us. It's not any more fair for you to take advantage of a man's vulnerability to mixed signals, hidden meanings, and mistaken illusions than it is for a man to take advantage of yours. Women are supposed to be better equipped to maintain the emotional stability of our relationships. Let's take advantage of that knowledge.

8
Special Techniques Your Mother Never Taught You

Your mother and grandmother were right about a lot of things that we modern women laughed at—until recently. After twenty years of feminism, the new morality, sharing feelings, sexual equality, open relationships, and other social experimentation, many women are beginning to realize that we may have given away the pot of gold before anyone got to the end of the rainbow. For most women, the rearranging of the sex roles served to confuse them, to make divorce easier (and more acceptable) for their husbands, to persuade them to have sex with men they didn't even like very much, and to do away with courtship, romance, and respect. Many women now feel they are paying a price for the freedom of the sexual revolution, and for many women the price is too high.

Men, on the other hand, have never had it so good. Before the sexual revolution they were expected to

123

court a woman and win her favors; now it's the other way around. Men are a hot commodity and women now chase after them. There isn't one woman over thirty reading this book who cannot honestly say that if she breaks up with her current lover, husband, or steady, there won't be a flock of eager women ready to take him on, no matter what his faults or flaws. But how many new men will be breaking down *her* door?

Liz and Greg finally decided to call it quits after two years of marriage. Liz is an exceptionally striking woman, and Greg, while not movie star material, is tall, slim, well-groomed, and attractive enough by most women's standards. Both are in their late thirties. After the breakup, Liz sat home alone or went out with her women friends on most weekends. But that wasn't by choice. Most of her friends were married and didn't know any good, available men to fix Liz up with. She went to a few singles affairs, but even though she is pretty, she found that there were many other women just as good-looking, all competing for the few attractive men who were there. Those men who did talk to her and with whom she exchanged cards said they would call, but never did. It's true, she could have called them, but Liz operates on the principle that when a man and woman meet, he will be the one to call if he's interested.

Greg, on the other hand, had no trouble meeting lovely new women. He, too, went to a few singles parties, but because he's a man and expected to make the first move, all he had to do was be charming to a few women, take their phone numbers, call them for a first date, and he was on his way. He was *expected* to be the aggressor. What was perfectly acceptable for him would be considered forward or aggressive for Liz. So while Liz sat home or went out with second-rate men just to keep up socially and despaired of ever meeting Mr. Right, Greg had plenty of available and highly eligible women to sift through until he found Ms. Right.

Yes, we know you're going to say that you have called a man up and that he has been delighted to hear from you. Maybe you invited him out, or maybe he even asked you for a date during that initial phone call. And most men we interviewed said they would be flattered to have a woman call them up and ask them out. So what's the problem?

Just this: when a man and woman meet, even after a five-minute conversation, he knows whether he is interested in her or not, and if he is, he will let her know it. If she has to call him and promote another meeting, it's a good bet that he wasn't *that* interested in her, and he's never going to be.

We have never known of a situation where the woman has chased after a man and ended up in a lasting relationship. And when we asked those men who told us how "delighted" they were *not* to have made the first move that led to their current or former serious love, all of them admitted it wasn't really the women who had done the chasing: every one of them had met or seen their lovers and pursued them. So even though men may say they are flattered by a woman's call and may, indeed, go out with her a few times, she's not the woman they are going to fall in love with unless after that first date *he* decides to pursue *her*.

WHEN YOU HAVE TO MAKE THE FIRST MOVE

All of this advice is intended for those situations where you have already met and have had a chance (even a few minutes) to size each other up. But what about pursuing someone you've never met? There is nothing wrong with pulling some strings to meet a man you have seen or heard about.

Lynn, a friend of ours, has a weekly cable television show, and many of the local public relations agents in town contact her regularly to book their clients. One of these agents, a personal friend of Lynn's, told her that she had a terrific, wealthy, single client she would love Lynn to meet, but she didn't feel she could mix business with pleasure and fix them up. So they decided to book the client—Peter—on the show to talk about his rise from rags to riches. Peter, an extremely successful businessman, also wrote poetry of which he was very proud. Coincidentally, Lynn, too, wrote poetry as a hobby. Her agent friend told Peter all about Lynn—how talented, how charming, how pretty she was. Peter was already primed to like Lynn when he guested on her show. And Lynn, of course, turned on the charm full volume. As Peter was leaving the studio, she scribbled him a clever poem (which she had composed and memorized the previous night) and told him to read it later. Then she waved good-bye and disappeared into the studio.

Peter, of course, was intrigued. He read the poem on the spot, was amused by it, and charmed by Lynn. He called her from his car phone to ask her to dinner. They are now married, and only Lynn and her friend know the full story of how they met. In this case, the plot worked, but ultimately, after the initial meeting, Lynn was on her own. If Peter hadn't asked her out after that interview, she would not have called him. We stick by the rule: maneuver, contrive, do whatever is necessary to meet a man, but after you have met, let him make the first advances. If *you* have to do it, nothing much will come of the relationship and you will be very disappointed.

PLAYING HARD TO GET: IT STILL WORKS

Men still like the thrill of the chase; they need to think they have captured a rare prize. No matter what they say, they don't want an overeager, needy woman. After the relationship gels, they want you to want them, but are put off by anxious women who want too much, too soon. Our mothers were right when they cautioned us to play hard to get. Have you noticed that almost invariably it's the men you *don't* want who pursue you? Very often, the man we try so hard to impress just doesn't seem to be interested, whereas the ones we are pleasant but indifferent to always come back for more.

Why? Because we put out subtle signals, ones we're not even aware of. If a woman seems too interested too soon, the man might be scared off, or he might sense her eagerness and decide that she's not a challenge. Probably, it's subconscious with him, too, but somehow he just doesn't find this woman exciting. The smart woman knows it's essential to keep a man off-balance. She is charming but rather elusive. The great temptresses of history, from Eve to Cleopatra to Josephine to the Duchess of Windsor, all knew this. They knew how to please, delight, cajole, entice, mystify, humor, and subtly manipulate men. Every woman who is greatly successful with men still plays by these rules, even if the game has grown more sophisticated. Most of the women we have met who are in successful marriages abide by these rules, even if to the outside world it seems as if the man is in charge. That's what she wants him to think.

It's always better for you to be the pursued rather than the pursuer. The kind of woman who is adored and put on a pedestal is the kind of woman who:

- Doesn't compromise her standards—she deserves the best and gets it.
- Loves and adores her man yet subtly reminds him that she *could* live without him.
- Never lets him take her for granted.
- Is warm and caring but seems to have a private inner core.

It's the paradoxical nature of man to want what he can't have or what's hard to get. Men are goal-oriented. They are taught from the moment they are born to strive, fight, challenge, accomplish, and win. In the old days, they fought duels for the honor of a fair maiden, and although modern life is much more complex and the sex lines have blurred somewhat, men basically haven't changed much. In fact, nothing has really changed emotionally between the sexes. Men still want to slay dragons and impress the unapproachable damsel. They still need the challenge of winning the fairest maiden in the land. Their egos still need constant priming.

Obviously, you aren't going to acquiesce to men in *all* areas of your life, particularly in business, where women have worked hard for equal jobs and equal pay. But sharp women realize that the boardroom is not the bedroom, and the rules of the game change once the business suit is shed.

MAKE EACH LOVE YOUR FIRST

When you do finally get into a sexual relationship with your lover, act as though he is the first man in your life. Dorothy, a widow who was happily married for ten years, says she always thinks like a virgin. In her mind, each love affair really *is* her first. She always acts a bit shy and girlish, and she really feels that way. We think this is excellent advice. No matter how many husbands or lovers you have had, no man likes to feel that he's one of the crowd. Remember a man's ego. Keep a vision of your Mr. Wonderful slaying the dragon to protect you, the blushing, fair maiden. That's the way most men would like to think of themselves, and of you.

Vivian learned this too late. She made the mistake of telling Sam, her fiancé, about all of the previous, rather exotic, sexual experiences she'd had since her divorce. At the time it seemed like fun, sharing their past sexual histories with each other. Sam had traveled abroad extensively and had sampled the local women wherever he went. Vivian hadn't been *that* experimental, but there was the time she accompanied a date to a nudist colony and the time she was talked into an evening at a "swing" club—to say nothing of a couple of other episodes that she blushed to think of now. Sure enough, the first time she and Sam had a fight, he brought up all her old affairs. He told her she was a tramp and couldn't be trusted. He shouted that anyone who had done what she had would screw around again in the future. Later, he apologized profusely and promised never to bring it up again. But the seeds of doubt had been planted, and the damage was irreversible. Things were never the same between them, and eventually they broke up. It's true that Sam was unfair in his attack, but Vivian had given him the ammunition. It is also true that Sam had been much more promiscuous in the past than Vivian, but that didn't occur to either of them. They were both programmed to believe that men are supposed to be that way and that women aren't. Sam was rather proud of his sexual history. Vivian was ashamed of hers, so she became the vulnerable one.

DEVELOPING A NEW SEXUAL RELATIONSHIP

In your first sexual encounter with a new man, let him take the lead. Then, unless he does something that physically, emotionally, or morally offends you, don't criticize his technique. Convince him that everything is wonderful. He'll be trying hard to please you, and in time he will learn how. In order to be a good lover in the future, it's important that he feels comfortable and successful now. After sex, flattery will get you everywhere. No man can be complimented too much about his sexual prowess. Afterglow sex talk is crucial to your relationship.

Don't let much time elapse between the first sexual encounter and the second. Schedule a repeat performance as soon as possible because the second experience, not the first, will be more likely to really cement the relationship—or to end it. The second time, you're both over your stage fright and are concentrating more on the pleasure, or inadequacy, of the act itself. Mr. Wonderful has satisfied his curiosity about your sexual mysteries and is, subconsciously perhaps, more interested this time in how *he* feels during sex with you. If you want to keep this man, make sure this second time feels terrific to him. You can act a bit less girlish and modest. Again, follow his lead, but compliment him profusely, telling him you've thought of nothing else since your initial encounter, he makes you feel sensational, and so on.

But remember, always hold back a little. Let him tell you how wonderful *you* are, let him set the next date and always wait for *him* to say, "I love you."

BEFORE YOU HEAR
WEDDING BELLS

The way you act after the first and second sexual encounters will either cement the relationship or cause it to flounder. It will also set the pattern for the future. Many women at this point make the mistake of hearing wedding bells and thinking the relationship is now permanently set. If you've made this mistake, then you're forgetting that sex means much more to a woman than it does to a man. Unless your man is already in love with you, has declared his intentions, and has shown, not through his words but through his actions, that he is really serious about you, having sex with him once or twice is not going to persuade him.

Even if he seems to be genuinely smitten, the following advice should be followed *without fail*. Whether you waited six months, six weeks, or six days to sleep with him, the advice is the same: do not appear overeager. Let him call you the morning after. Do not call him first. Let him be the one to ask to see you again. Do not talk about the future unless he brings it up and, even then, be pleasantly noncommittal. Talk about *your* future plans—the trip you're planning to take next summer to visit your mother, the high school reunion in a distant city that you're looking forward to. Of course, if he suggests it, you can make vague future plans with him, too, but until he commits himself to the relationship, subtly let him know you have a full life without him.

After you have had sex a few times, and even though you are seeing each other exclusively, it's a good idea to be unexpectedly busy one night when he calls. You might invent a business dinner, an evening with an out-of-town friend, or a visit to the bedside of a hospitalized coworker—whatever sounds legitimate and nonthreatening. In fact, you should really plead nonavailability for a couple of nights that he wants to see you. Be charming, apologetic, warm, and loving on the phone—but be busy. Never let him feel absolutely sure of you. Even though he can't put his finger on it by anything you say, you want him to feel a little off-balance. You want him to feel that he doesn't quite have you yet and that he must work harder (be kinder, more attentive, more loving, more available) to win you fully. Remember, men like the thrill of the chase. Don't make things too easy.

Olga learned this lesson the hard way. She wanted so much to love and be loved that she practically threw herself at any man who seemed interested in her. She went to bed with them when *they* were ready and convinced herself that she really wanted it, too. After one or two dates, she would invariably ask the man over for a gourmet meal in her immaculate apartment. She sent them amusing cards, bought them little nonsense gifts, catered to their needs, entertained their friends and/or children, and was always available. Any man would fall in love with Olga, wouldn't he? The perfect woman, you would think. Well, you would be wrong. Men kept disappointing Olga, and she didn't know why. One man after another would go with her for a while and then disappear from her life. She couldn't see that she was being too eager, too willing. Not only was she scaring them off with all that undeserved attention, but she had removed all the obstacles from their courtship.

They didn't have to do much of anything to get her undivided attention. It was all too easy, and somehow these men would stop finding Olga exciting.

We asked her to try an experiment with the next eligible man she met; try it our way. A few months later, she called with some good news. She had met Dave at a lecture. They went out for coffee afterward and talked for two hours. By the time she got home, his call was already on her answering machine. The old Olga would have returned the call immediately, even if it was 1:00 A.M. The new Olga waited until late the next day to return the call. When he asked her out for that night, Olga very apologetically said she already had plans, and then suggested a night later that week. Dave reluctantly agreed and said he hated to wait that long to see her again. When they finally went out, Olga did not get romantic, did not suggest seeing him again, but just waited for him to make the next move.

She didn't have to wait long. Dave was enthusiastically making plans for them for the coming weekend. Olga agreed only to Saturday, and by the end of the day, he was thoroughly smitten. Olga told him then that she didn't want to get into a heavy relationship, but she did enjoy his company *so* much that she would break her own rule and maybe see him two or three times a week. Her attitude only spurred him on to more pursuit, and he couldn't do enough for her. He called her twice a day. He bought her flowers. He bought her little gifts. He even cooked dinner for *her*. She told us she had never been treated so well by a man, and she agreed that holding back certainly worked for her. It went against her nature, but the rewards were well worth the effort.

It will work for you, too. Most men are suspicious of things that come too easily. Maybe it's their work ethic, but they seem to put more value on things they have to work for.

This technique should not be confused with coldness; you must remain warm and approachable as you keep your distance. Southern women have the technique down to perfection. If you know any, study the way they act around men; they should give lessons in flattery, coquettishness, charm—and subtle manipulation. Southern belles have been called "iron butterflies," and "iron fists in velvet gloves," and the descriptions are very apt. These women know what they want, and they know how to get it. No matter what their age, their manner around men is awesome. They seem to be very sure of themselves as they laugh, flirt, and gently tease men. Underlying their entire being is an air of feminine sexuality. Strong men are easily reduced to putty around these women.

LEARNING TO LAUGH

Humor is another powerful technique. Our mothers said it again: "Laugh and the world laughs with you." You should always maintain a sense of humor, a sense of the ridiculous, around men. Every man we spoke with mentioned a sense of humor as a definite turn-on. Many men complain that women take themselves too seriously, are too easily upset, and turn trifles into major events. You'll probably agree that there is some truth to this and, yes, you've been guilty, too—sometimes we forget that most of today's problems will be yesterday's bad memories. Men want to be around a woman who's fun and who doesn't take herself, or the world, too seriously.

Humor is also a wonderful way to lighten up a tense situation or end an argument. It's awfully difficult to stay angry at someone who's lighthearted and amusing. If you're the one who is angry, a cheery sense of humor is going to unnerve your man a lot more than tears and screaming. Anger and yelling he might expect; humor and good cheer he doesn't. If he does something wrong and, instead of showing anger you are amused, pleasant, and off-hand about the whole thing, he will feel a lot more guilty than he would if you threw a tantrum. And he will bend over backward to make it up to you—short of apologizing, that is.

Most men find it almost impossible to say the three little words *I am sorry*, so don't press it. He'll make it up in other ways, and actions do speak louder than words. Remember, it's what your man does on a steady basis that counts. Of course, if he says, "I love you," or "I am sorry," accompanied by the appropriate actions, that's extra frosting.

So, if your man does something crummy, don't yell; try a little cheer instead. Nancy learned this when two different dates made practically the same social error on two different occasions. She handled each incident differently and the results were astonishing. In the first episode, she had asked an old flame, Rodney, to see a special screening of a major movie on his birthday and then go out for dinner. He was delighted to accept. She was half-hoping to rekindle the romance and was looking forward to the evening with great anticipation.

The screening was exactly at six-thirty—if you are not there on time, the doors are closed and no one is admitted after the movie has begun. Nancy made a special point of telling this to Rodney when they made the date. She rushed home from work, battled the freeway traffic, barely had time to dress and redo her makeup, and was ready and eager at six o'clock. Rodney, a writer, worked at home and did not have any set hours or any boss looking over his shoulder.

Six-fifteen came and went. Then six-twenty. Then six-twenty-five. Nancy was steaming by this time, mentally calling Rodney every name she could think of. How could he be so inconsiderate, so ungrateful? She was both angry and worried that something terrible had happened to him. What else could have delayed him so dramatically? Finally, at six-twenty-five, the bell rang, and there stood Rodney, sheepishly explaining that he was delayed in terrible traffic!

Well, of course, Nancy lit into him. How could he be so inconsiderate! Why didn't he make allowances for traffic? He didn't even have a good excuse! Didn't he realize that she was upset and worried? And on and on. Of course, the more she raved, the stonier Rodney became and the less guilty he felt. They raced to the car and tried to make the screening, but of course, they were much too late.

Now they weren't speaking to each other, neither one of them felt like eating, and the evening was pretty well ruined. Eventually, they made up enough to get through dinner, but the flame not only wasn't rekindled that night, it remained permanently out.

You might be thinking that Rodney deserved it. After all, he was inconsiderate, and it was his fault the evening was a disaster. That may be true, but Nancy wanted something: a romantic reunion with Rodney. He was usually fairly punctual, so this was not a habitual thing. Was the movie really that important if she was playing for bigger stakes? To save her relationship with Rodney, she could have reacted much differently.

A few months later, she got the chance to test her new theory. She received complimentary tickets to a play and invited Marty, a man she had recently met, to accompany her. The play started at seven-thirty and they planned to leave at seven and have a bite afterward.

Seven came and went. Then seven-fifteen. Then seven-twenty-five. Nancy couldn't believe it. It was an instant replay of her disastrous evening with Rodney! But this time, she decided to play the scenario much differently. At seven-thirty, a red-faced, apologetic Marty appeared, begging mercy for his lateness. There was a long-distance phone call, trouble starting his car, traffic. Instead of angry accusations or even a cutting remark, Nancy smiled pleasantly and told him that it didn't matter a bit—she was just so glad he wasn't in an accident. The play got lousy reviews, anyway, and they could always see it another time. He was so grateful he almost melted. The evening went like a dream, Marty couldn't do enough for her.

At the end of the evening, he apologized again for his tardiness, told Nancy what a great sport she was, and promised to make it up to her on their next date. Of course, Marty should not have been so late, and Nancy wouldn't put up with such behavior on a regular basis. But what did she have to lose this one time by being pleasant instead of petulant? She had everything to gain!

You can use humor and good nature to get you out of any tight spot. If a man gets too familiar too soon and sprouts a case of wandering hands, stop him with a funny remark. If he gets angry at the waiter and starts bellowing in the restaurant, say something ridiculous. If he is annoyed at something you've done, break the tension with a smile. It's very difficult to stay angry at someone who responds with humor.

LEAVE 'EM WANTING MORE

There are some other techniques that work to keep
you in control of the relationship. One of the most
important is based on a well-known showbiz truism:
"Always leave the audience wanting more." In the
case of your relationship, the way to accomplish this
is to always be the one to end the conversation, say
good-bye on the telephone, break from an embrace,
disentangle after sex. It's a very, very subtle form of
rejection, and it will definitely make the man subconsciously feel that he wants more. Think about
your past or present relationships. Who usually ends
the phone calls? Who usually breaks first from a
sexual encounter? If you smoke, who usually is the
first to light up a cigarette after sex? We bet it's the
man.

Start making a conscious effort to notice this part
of your relationship, and begin making changes.
You'll notice a difference in his attitude very soon.

Betty used this knowledge to make a change in her
relationship with Steve, who is a compulsive worka-
holic. She understood that a man dedicated to his
work is not going to be as emotionally available as
she would have liked, but still, she didn't want to be
treated as part of the furniture. Steve was faithful,
punctual, and reliable, yet he didn't seem to really
need her. He didn't call her every day—*she* called
him. He didn't initiate sex most of the time—*she* did.
When he was out of town on one of his frequent
business trips, he rarely called her. And when they
did talk on the phone, he was always in a hurry to get
off. Instead of nagging, complaining, or restating her
needs, Betty decided to try the holding-back technique.

She let a couple of days go by and did not call

Steve. Eventually, of course, he called her. She was
warm, friendly, happy to hear from him, but she was
in such a hurry, just rushing out the door. She would
talk to him tomorrow. And then she hung up quickly
and turned on her answering machine. She did not
call him the next day. That night, he called her and
she wasn't home. The message he left on her machine
was *very* warm, reminding her they had a date the
next night. He called her the following day at her
office to make sure she had gotten the message and
to set a time. Again, she was warm, vivacious, sweet,
but very rushed: "Can't talk now, honey. See you
tonight." By this time, Steve had called *her* three days
in a row and was reminding *her* about their date.
That evening, Betty made sure to break from their
hello embrace first. At the restaurant, when he took
her hand, she withdrew it casually after a few minutes.

She practiced this technique all evening, whenever
the moment seemed right. For a change, she made no
sexual move toward Steve, but he could hardly wait
to get her inside the door, he was so ardent. He
certainly initiated sex that night! Afterward, she let
just enough time elapse, then got up and disappeared
into the bathroom, telling Steve she'd be back in a
minute. When she did return, Steve was intently
peering into space. Instead of asking him what he
was thinking, as she would have done previously, she
said nothing and just cuddled up beside him. Steve
told her he felt he'd been neglecting her lately and
asked why they didn't definitely plan that vacation to
Hawaii she had mentioned? Betty could hardly believe her ears. She had been lobbying for them to get
away together for six months to no avail. But instead
of hugging and kissing Steve in delight at the suggestion, as she really wanted to do, Betty gently put her

arm around him and said she would just love to go away but she was starting a new project at the office and didn't know if or when she could get time off. Of course, now Steve was more determined than ever to go. She promised to see if she could work things out and to let him know in a few days.

Clearly, Betty had very subtly changed the balance of power in the relationship. By using the holding-back technique, she had forced Steve to come after her instead of the other way around. She continued to employ this strategy, and eventually Steve was calling her regularly and treating her much more romantically. He seemed to have more respect for her in general. Their sex life improved immeasurably also. What had happened was really very simple: as Betty pulled back, Steve pushed forward to fill the void. Betty was practicing a very subtle form of psychic rejection, and although Steve couldn't actually see or identify it, he could feel it. Her holding back made him feel not quite so sure of her, so in order not to lose her love, he was forced to think of her more often, phone her more, and be more affectionate and loving.

LET HIM COME TO YOU

Another behavioral strategy is the push-pull technique. The next time you are in a crowded restaurant, look around at all the couples. In most instances, you will see one person leaning in and the other person leaning back. The body language will show that one person is giving, (talking, laughing, questioning, entertaining) and the other is accepting, (responding, listening, smiling). The one leaning in is trying harder to interest the one leaning back. Nine times out of ten, the person leaning forward is the woman. When two women eat together, they either both lean in or both lean back, unless one is trying to sell or convince the other of something, in which case the one who is selling leans in.

The next time you are on a date, try an experiment. Stop talking, sweetly close your mouth, and lean back in your chair. And wait. Pretty soon your date will lean forward and start "selling" to you. Very few people can tolerate silence in a nonsilent atmosphere, so someone has to fill it in. If it's not you, then it will be him. Respond, of course, but keep the distance. Don't lean forward. Let him come to you.

This also works at cocktail parties. Let him be the one to move toward you if you start a conversation. Don't invade his space; let him invade yours, and then casually step back a little while you keep up the conversation. In effect, you will be drawing him to you. This works only if you know you are in control. If it's a new man, if you just feel like flirting a little, or if you're unsure of his intentions toward you, then use the following version of space invasion.

We all have a comfort zone in relation to other people. When two strangers are alone together on an elevator, they usually stand as far apart as physically possible. If the entering person stands right next to the person already in the elevator, that person will invariably move away, uncomfortable at having his or her space invaded. The same is true for positioning in an almost empty movie theatre, or even on a park bench. We are all surrounded by invisible lines that protect us from too much intimacy from strangers.

This concept of space is a fascinating subject, and once you understand it, you can use it to your advantage with men. Two women talking together at a cocktail party are comfortable standing very close to one another. A just-introduced man and woman are comfortable with much more distance between them. If one moves closer to the other and there is no reason or desire for sexual overtures, then the one whose space has been invaded becomes uncomfortable and backs away.

On the other hand, if there is a spark of mutual interest (even unconsciously), then when one moves in closer, both will find it comfortable to remain that way. The same is true of casual touching—of a hand or an arm or a shoulder—or other gestures that suggest intimacy. They will be welcomed if both parties are interested. If one or the other is unavailable or not interested, then he or she will feel uncomfortable and off-balance, and will back off.

If you meet a man in whom you're interested, try the space technique. Invade his space, just a little, and wait to see what happens. If he holds his ground, or even comes forward to meet you, he's probably interested. By entering his space, you have made him *very* aware of you and have shown him you're interested.

The next thing you can do is casually touch him on the hand while he lights your cigarette or brings you a drink, or on the arm if you're engaged in conversation or laughing with him. You can engage in these techniques—space invading, space retreating, and intimate touching—any place, any time. They work at parties, on dates, with new men and old flames. They're part of the basic ground rules of flirting and female seduction. It's fun to do, so start practicing at the next party you attend, and watch what happens!

9
First-Night Etiquette

Your instincts and common sense should tell you when the time is right for sex. That first physical encounter could very well be the turning point in your relationship. With a highly sexual man, it can be a powerful incentive in cementing the relationship if a strong foundation has already been established.

Plan your night very carefully. You are starring in this production, so don't leave anything to chance. Impromptu, explosive sex where two people just look at each other, gasp, fall into each other's arms, couple in wild abandonment, and achieve mutual orgasm to the sound of Ravel's "Bolero" is wonderful and exciting. But, unfortunately, it usually doesn't happen that way, especially the first time. And if you are not one of the rare few to whom this miracle of chemistry happens, you will want to leave very little to chance when it comes to this important turning point in your relationship.

Now is the time to put away the ghosts of the past.

Your new lover is not your former husband. He is a different person with his own unique approaches and responses. He will feel, taste, smell, and act differently. Forget comparisons, good or bad. This is the man you have chosen to be your new mate. Concentrate solely on him—and on the two of you together.

We are assuming that you have set the emotional foundation for this relationship, so let's talk about how you can make the first night an experience that he will never forget.

Try not to plan it on a week night, when you both have to think about going to work the next day. Although we advise *not* spending the whole night together that first time, you will both be more relaxed if you have the weekend to look forward to.

Don't leave that crucial first time together up to chance, or even to the man with whom you will share it. It is up to you to make it perfect. Suggest an evening that has romantic overtones, an atmosphere of intimacy, and an agenda you can control. If you think that romantic music, candlelight, and good food and wine seem too contrived and corny, think again. There is a reason why those accoutrements have been part of the mating ritual for centuries. They set a mood that inspires intimacy. An evening at the bowling alley, rushing to make a curtain for a play, or attending a big social gathering are not good preludes to good first-time sex. Neither are movies and concerts where there's very little interaction between the two of you, or spending the evening with another couple. The preamble to that crucial first time together should be a romantic, playful, relaxed, and private time.

Don't make the same mistake as our friend Randi. After almost two months of dating a man she was really crazy about, Randi decided that the Saturday night of their two-month anniversary would be a wonderful and meaningful time for their first sexual experience. They spent a glorious day at the beach, jogging in the surf and taking in the sun. They met some friends for a couple of sets of tennis. Then they all hurried home to shower and meet for dinner back at the beach. It was a beautiful, warm, balmy evening, and there was even a full moon. Everything seemed perfect between Randi and her man. There was just the right amount of sexual tension. They couldn't keep their hands off each other all evening, and they both knew what would happen when they got home.

During the drive back from dinner at the beach, they held hands and listened to music, but the traffic was heavy, and they were both getting drowsy.

By the time they arrived at her house it was getting late, and they were both a little irritable from the combination of jogging, lying in the sun, and all the driving back and forth to the beach. Randi sensed that it would be better to wait until they were both in a better frame of mind, but the expectation had been building all evening, and they both felt almost obligated to make love. As you might guess, it was a disaster. She was sunburned and irritable. He was overtired and had trouble getting an erection. They finally consummated the act, but it was a disappointment for both of them.

YOUR PLACE OR HIS?

This decision can make or break your first night together. In most cases, you will be much better off if it happens at your place. That way, you can set the stage to your own advantage. In the beginning, one of you is going to feel somewhat uncomfortable. Men can handle this more easily because they have fewer accessories to worry about. It's a little ridiculous for a mature woman to pack up her makeup, hair rollers, robe, and so forth and schlepp it along on a date. It's more than awkward to cross a man's threshold carrying your overnight case—even if it *is* a Gucci!

You will feel much more confident in your own surroundings, where you can control the lighting, the telephone, and who comes wandering in at inopportune moments. You'll be much more comfortable on your own turf and in your own bed, where you'll be able to slip away and find the bathroom without tripping over obstacles and going into the closet by mistake. You will also feel much more alluring if you are able to neaten your smeared makeup and freshen your face and body, and you will feel and look much more attractive if you are able to slip into a beautiful robe and sexy peignoir than back into your pantyhose, underwear, and crumpled clothes.

One negative aspect of being at your place is that it is a little more difficult to end the evening without spending the night together. It is *not* recommended that you spend all night together after that first sexual encounter. You want him to remember the magic of the night, not morning breath, tangled hair, smeared mascara, rumpled sheets, and other realities of the morning after. A friend told us about the time she spent a wonderful first night with her boyfriend at his hilltop townhouse. They cooked dinner together and dined overlooking the lights of the city. The house was almost all glass and the view was magnificent. After dinner, they danced while the lights twinkled all around them. The finale was making love in front of the fire, suspended in that glass treehouse. They fell asleep afterward, still curled up on the plush carpet and nestled in the pillows in front of the fireplace.

When they awoke the next morning, the bright sun was pouring in the uncurtained glass walls from all sides, and they were surrounded by empty wine glasses, scattered coffee cups, and rumpled clothes. Our friend glanced in the mirror over the fireplace and practically cried when she saw how she looked. He didn't look so great, either, in the harsh light of morning. Of course, seeing someone you care about in less than perfect circumstances isn't going to ruin a romance. But it would have been so much better if our friend had been able to leave him that night with the memory of that magical evening and the way she looked in front of the fire, against the lights of the city.

WHAT YOU PROBABLY DIDN'T THINK OF

To return to the practical for a moment, even if the scene is set to perfection and the mood conducive to romance, there are numerous nitty-gritty details to which you should give some thought. Take out your contact lenses, use waterproof mascara instead of false eyelashes, and forego a girdle for the evening. These are all seemingly minor nuisances, but they can cause some very awkward moments if you don't consider them.

If you need a wig because of hair loss, tell the man about it long before you are ready for sex with him. Even the most loving and accepting man would probably be nonplussed by starting the evening with a partner with a head full of hair and ending it in bed with a bald one. Straightforwardness is the only way to handle it. When your relationship has endured the test of time, you will probably feel comfortable removing the wig for a night. But in the beginning, most women feel more seductive and sensual leaving it on. There are fixatives that should be able to withstand even the most vigorous lovemaking.

As for hairpieces, it's best to keep your hairdo simple when you suspect the evening will lead to bed. Save the wiglets and falls for a more formal occasion.

Since you've been married before, you surely don't need a lesson on contraception. But if you haven't dated for the last ten years or so, you'll find that some things have definitely changed. Herpes (which isn't fatal but has no cure), the venereal diseases, and AIDS, have changed the sexual mores of most single men and women and forced everyone to think more than twice about our sexual partners. We cannot emphasize strongly enough the following advice. ***You are taking a risk if you have sex without insisting that the man use a condom, unless you know the past history of everyone he has slept with for the last seven to ten years.*** It is a very delicate and touchy subject to introduce with the man of your dreams, but unless you know him *very* well and have known him for a very long time, it is in your best interests *and* his to tactfully suggest he use a condom. Many women keep one in their wallets or on a bedside table, just in case he doesn't have his own. As embarrassing as it seems, if you tell him in a loving and honest way that it is for your mutual protection, an understanding and sensible man will not be offended. Don't go into long apologies and explanations. Just make it as unobtrusive as possible. Help him with it, and be warm and loving. Make a joke out of rolling on the condom—make it seem sort of silly but cute. And then forget about it.

As for your own birth control (most women feel

unsafe just relying on that condom), don't ever be embarrassed to excuse yourself and use it—you must! You'll be a lot more embarrassed if you have to tell your new man that you're pregnant.

SO YOUR BODY ISN'T PERFECT: WHOSE IS?

Many women wonder how to handle a first sexual experience with a man if they have had a mastectomy or colostomy or if they have extremely disfiguring scars. In this case, honesty is always the best policy. You shouldn't be going to bed with a man before you have established enough of a relationship to feel comfortable telling him about your physical condition. It's not something you can camouflage, like acne or age spots. It is part of what he will have to love and accept in order to accept and love you. If he can't (and some people just aren't emotionally capable of handling this type of thing), then the relationship isn't meant to be. You should discuss any physical problems long before your first night together.

When it comes to camouflaging minor figure flaws, don't worry if your body is not perfect. His probably isn't, either. The way you respond to him and make him feel is far more important then being a perfect ten. It doesn't hurt, though, to have low-watt light bulbs in your bedside lamp, fresh sheets on the bed, a couple of candles glowing, and some soft, romantic music. Pitch-dark rooms lend more of a sordid, rather than sensuous, atmosphere. Just the right amount of soft, warm candlelight will melt away whatever traces of cellulite may be lurking in those seldom displayed areas.

FINALLY,
LET YOURSELF GO

From here on you shouldn't be thinking of anything except the wonderful things the two of you are doing with each other. You should be practicing the wonderfully rewarding art of sexual surrender.

As we all know, even with the most careful planning and the greatest desire, the first time is often not the greatest. You are both nervous, anxious to please, and worried about performance. Men especially are plagued by performance anxiety. Don't take it personally if he can't consummate the act on the first try. It doesn't mean you don't turn him on or that you are doing anything wrong. Don't make a big deal about it. Don't assure him that it doesn't matter, because it does to *him*, very much. Just be gentle and loving and seductively murmur some of the things that are going well. Tell him you love his skin, the feel of his muscles, the way he smells, the way he caresses you—all of the positive things that you *do* feel at the moment. We aren't writing a sex manual, but there are plenty of them on the market that can teach you how to be great in bed from a purely physical viewpoint. Concentrate on the more subtle emotions involved in sexuality. In the long run, they are far more important than technique. Make him feel good *emotionally*, and he will be back for more of *you*, not just sex.

This may sound appalling to you, but on the first sexual occasion, you will be doing yourself and your relationship a favor if you fake orgasm (assuming, of course, it doesn't happen naturally). That's right, we actually said *"fake orgasm!"*

This is not to suggest a lifetime devoid of sexual

fulfillment or a relationship built on dishonesty. The point is, men are very sensitive about their ability to sexually satisfy women. Most men do not understand or believe that a woman can enjoy sex thoroughly without having an orgasm every time. Men place a great deal of pride in their sexual abilities, and when they don't feel they are sexually satisfying with a woman, they tend to feel inadequate and embarrassed. No one likes to be around someone with whom they feel inadequate and embarrassed. So, they are likely to move on before your sexual relationship has a chance to become fully developed.

Faking orgasm in the beginning of a love affair doesn't mean you will never have an orgasm with that person. It just means that you may be buying a little time to further cement all the aspects of your relationship, as you develop your sexual knowledge of your partner. It means you are making the man feel strong and successful in an area that is of prime importance to him.

It doesn't even mean you have to lie. If he is insecure enough to ask if you were satisfied, there are plenty of ways to suggest that you were without directly saying, "Yes, I had an orgasm." "You are wonderful," "I feel like I'm floating," "It's so wonderful to be in your arms," and similar statements, when whispered between kisses and sighs, are all wonderfully assuring.

After you have established a comfortable sexual intimacy, there are many ways to let a man know what turns you on in bed. We don't mean barking directions or making an anonymous gift of *How to Make Love to a Woman*. If you use positive reinforcement with a man and subtly guide his lovemaking by what you do to him, you will find that most men will get the message. And remember, if you focus in on your feelings, open your mind to your own sensuality, and let your subconscious instincts guide you, it won't be long until faking an orgasm will no longer be an issue.

10
Surefire Tips on Taking a Trip with a Man

No matter how well you think you know your lover, you won't really know each other and the full scope of each other's habits and idiosyncrasies until you take a trip together. You've heard the old adage, "You never know a man until you've lived with him." We would broaden that to, "You never know a man until you've taken a trip with him." Even long-married couples who get along reasonably well in the comfort of their own home and predictable daily routine find that traveling can be stressful on their relationship.

There's the new experience of being together all day, every day. Some people find their relationship can't stand so much togetherness. And a multitude of things can go wrong on a trip: lost luggage, canceled flights, car breakdowns, dishonored hotel reservations, foreign language problems, unfamiliar food, sickness, bad weather, terrible accommodations, wrong clothes, and the list goes on. We hope your romantic holiday is as smooth as silk, but any number of disasters can happen. How you and he react can make or break your budding romance.

Probably, you learned a lot from your previous marriage. Think back over the trips you took with your husband. Didn't things go wrong that could have been avoided by better planning? Or when they did go unavoidably wrong despite your best efforts, wasn't there a better way you could have handled the situation?

Marge had been dating Bud about six months. They thought they had an intimate relationship. Like many typical, hard-working young couples, they saw each other about twice during the week and spent weekends together, sleeping mostly at Marge's apartment. They weren't actually alone together that much, though, since they were always busy doing something. They went out to dinner, to football games, to plays, to friends' homes. On Saturdays, they did errands and then maybe saw a movie. Except for an occasional Sunday night, they never spent many waking hours together alone at home. When they took a two-week vacation together at Club Med, they looked forward to it with excited anticipation.

But Marge and Bud had never traveled together before and didn't know each other's travel styles. Bud thought Marge took way too much luggage, and he found she was a very nervous traveler. She checked and double-checked the tickets, insisted on getting to the airport two hours ahead of time, worried about the location of their seats, and when finally aloft, was a nervous wreck every time the plane hit an air pocket.

Bud, on the other hand, was calm, cool, and collected. Because his travel style was "easy come, easy go," Marge's hypersensitivity grated on him. She, however, felt that he should be more soothing and helpful. The trip did not get off to an auspicious beginning for either of them.

Things got worse at Club Med. The second day, Marge badly sprained her ankle. The fourth day, she developed "la tourista." There she was with a bum ankle and a worse stomach. All she could do was stay in bed and wish she were dead. Bud, on the other hand, felt fine. The sun was shining, the surf was up, the palm trees were swaying, and the music was playing. He tried to be as helpful as he knew how to be: he brought Marge food and drink, looked in on her several times a day, didn't stay out late (although he did go to the disco every night), and inquired solicitously about her welfare. When her tourista subsided, he helped her hobble to the beach, propped her up on a lounge, and checked on her often. He did the same for her at night at the disco. Bud didn't see why he shouldn't dance and have fun with his new-found friends just because Marge couldn't. After all, he did keep checking on her, bringing her drinks, and occasionally sitting at the table with her.

Well, the postscript to this story is that Marge felt neglected and ignored by Bud. She felt that he did only what *had* to be done—what he would have done even for a male friend he was vacationing with. She didn't feel he treated her as a woman he loved. When they returned to the city, she told him off. They had a major argument and she broke off their relationship. Bud didn't think he had done anything wrong, but he was glad it was over. He had seen a side of Marge he didn't like.

It doesn't matter who was or wasn't right; the point is that Marge and Bud really didn't know each other at all before they went away. Their six-month relationship had been emotionally superficial, and when out-of-the-ordinary problems occurred on their vacation, they couldn't cope with each other.

Jenny and Grant went to Puerto Rico for a week. During the four months they had been together, Jenny had been impressed by Grant's take-charge attitude toward life. He seemed to be able to handle anything. At restaurants he always demanded and got the best table. Commandeering taxis was no challenge to him, and somehow they never had to wait in line for anything. Jenny immensely enjoyed Grant's wielding of power because she also benefited from it and was treated royally.

On the Puerto Rican junket, however, Jenny began to see Grant in a different light. Back home in the city, she only saw him at night in a social setting. Now she was with him every minute, and as she saw how he acted on planes and trains, how he spoke to the desk clerk at hotels, and how he handled waiters and sight-seeing guides, Jenny began to perceive that Grant was a pompous, overbearing boor. He talked too loudly, was rude to people who didn't speak English, and insisted on having his way even if it was contrary to the customs of this different culture. While Grant was concerned for Jenny's every comfort, he wasn't interested in her sight-seeing suggestions. They went to restaurants *he* picked, on excursions *he* planned. Jenny soon realized that if she continued this relationship, she would be swallowed up and have no life of her own. One week alone with Grant in Puerto Rico had shown her more about him than months of Saturday night dating ever would.

It works the other way, too. Any personality flaws *you* have will show up all too glaringly on that first trip together. A trip together is instant, forced intimacy; that's hard enough with a woman friend, let alone a lover. Have you ever gone away with a

woman friend you thought was a great companion
and found out you couldn't stand her by the end of
the trip? People seem to show the worst side of themselves in different surroundings. Or maybe they were
really like that all the time, and you just never noticed it in the familiarity of your ordinary surroundings.

At home you usually live in more than one room,
but on a trip you are thrown together in one small
hotel room, sharing one inadequate bathroom (a
suite with two baths is great if you can swing it).
Suddenly, there the two of you are, facing that king-
sized bed, eyeing that mini-sized closet and feeling
slightly naughty and a little embarrassed (yes, it's
natural to feel that way, even if you practically live
together at home). The surroundings are strange, the
situation is strained, and you feel a little out of
control. Here is where a sense of humor can really
make a difference. Say something funny, make a big
deal out of trying out the bed, or give your lover a
cute surprise gift you brought along to mark the
occasion—a wild pair of undershorts, a silly and
appropriate card, scented massage oil, or anything
that is symbolic or funny to the two of you. That will
break the tension and start things out on a light
note.

BEFORE YOU SAIL
AROUND THE WORLD

Your best bet is to start off with a weekend trip
before working your way up to that grand European
tour. The weekend will establish your habits together and yet allow you to relax, because you know
it's short. Even if things don't work out, you can exit
much more gracefully later because you know you

will only have to be gracious for a couple of days. It would be disastrous to be in a foreign land with a man you found you didn't like, knowing you're dependent on him for the next three weeks.

That happened to a recently divorced friend of ours who had been dating a very wealthy older man. David invited Sally on a trip to Italy. She had never been abroad and was naturally very excited. He lived in a neighboring city, so Sally saw him only on weekends. This was to be their first trip away together. Not only was Sally excited about seeing Italy, she also looked forward to spending time with David and getting to know him better.

She got to know him better, all right—to her dismay. Sally found out that David was stingy, inflexible, and very eccentric. They stayed at a third-class hotel that he called "quaint" and Sally called "rundown." Although they were on vacation, David adhered to a very rigid schedule: up at 7:00, lunch at 1:00, dinner at 8:00, bed at 11:00. He didn't want to sightsee with Sally because he'd seen it all before. So after a few days, Sally reluctantly decided to go off on her own and join some day tours. David often wanted to eat in the room or skip dinner altogether. Some days he would get up early and disappear for most of the day. All of this made Sally very uncomfortable and anxious. Here she was in a strange country where she knew no one. She was completely at the mercy of David, who was turning out to be a very unpleasant companion. This certainly wasn't the romantic, exotic vacation she had planned on. To top things off, he had possession of their tickets home and Sally couldn't afford to buy her own ticket and leave. So Sally had to stick out the three weeks; she returned with the advice that no woman should ever go farther than a hundred miles away from home on her first trip with a man.

On the other hand, if the vibes are right and you both handle things well, every kind of disaster can occur, and you will come home closer that ever.

Leslie went away to an island in the Caribbean with Bruce, a man she was seeing quite seriously at the time. A series of disasters befell them. For some reason, all the water on the island was cut off and the only water they had—for bathing, brushing their teeth, and flushing the toilet—was what they could fill the bathtub with once a day. That meant no nice long showers together, only a quick sponge with soapy washcloth. They could only flush the toilets once a day (a problem they solved by using the rest rooms in the casino and lobby most of the time). It was not a comfortable situation, but they decided it was funny and began to laugh about making do. They could have left, of course, but they were having too much fun. Bruce drove into town and surprised Leslie with a case of bottled water. Then she got sick, developing a high fever, stomach pains, chills—the works. Bruce took charge, called the hotel manager, found a local doctor, persuaded him to come to their room, filled her prescriptions, and spent the night wrapping her in blankets and holding her hand.

The next day she was much better and knew at least that she would live! She encouraged Bruce to go out and have some fun, but before he did, he called the desk to tell them she was sick in the room and ask them to check on her periodically. When he returned that evening (with a bouquet of flowers), they had dinner in the room—Leslie looking pale and disheveled, eating Jell-O and ginger ale, Bruce looking healthy and exuberant, eating steak and regaling her with stories of his day's explorations. Sick as she was, they were actually having fun!

By the end of the trip they felt very close to each other. They both admired the way the other had reacted in adverse circumstances, and they had established real intimacy.

FOOLPROOF TIPS ON TAKING A TRIP

Never go away with a man you haven't been sexually intimate with for a while. If you don't heed this advice, you might find yourself in our friend Jane's situation. She accepted a tennis weekend with a nice guy she'd been out with only twice. After several sets of singles and a candlelight dinner, they finally were alone, facing a king-sized bed. Things proceeded as expected until the moment of culmination, at which point Jane realized her partner had some kinky sexual preferences. She was no prude, but it was clear to both of them that their tastes were vastly different, and they both ended up embarrassed and frustrated. Needless to say, the trip was ruined for Jane. She was stuck many miles from home and had no choice but to wait out the weekend. If she had discovered his desires on her own turf, she could have handled the situation gracefully and gone home to her own bed.

The first time, make it a two- or three-day weekend. Stay fairly close to home, no more than a few hours by plane or car. If you are flying, keep your own ticket with you. If you are driving, take your credit card, driver's license, and enough money for emergencies. Unless you like the thrill of the unknown, be sure to make hotel reservations in advance. Decide, in advance, who's going to pay for what. If you pay your own way, you're on much more of an equal footing in making decisions. Discuss in advance your possible differences in sleeping habits, privacy needs, routines, and so forth. How will you handle things if you're a night person and he's a day person, for example? Does your reading in bed keep him awake? Will his rustling around getting dressed early in the morning disturb you? What if he's a fresh air freak and insists on throwing the window wide open? Keep in mind, you usually have only one ordinary size room to maneuver in. Remember to take along any pills or medicines you might need. It's a good idea to bring along a small emergency kit containing aspirin, bandages, antacid, antibiotic ointment, vaseline, and the like, as well as safety pins and needle and thread.

Register under your own name. No one cares, and you'll feel like a kept woman if you register as Mr. and Mrs. when you aren't, and even worse if you don't register at all.

A newly divorced friend of ours was really embarrassed when she went away with a man for the first time. She was used to registering as Mr. and Mrs., and she was ashamed to be looked on as some man's girlfriend. So she requested that he sign in as Mr. and Mrs. Jim Woodley. It just so happened his ex-wife was staying at this resort also, and the desk clerk, confused by two Mrs. Woodleys, mixed up their calls.

Atmosphere can definitely make or break this first trip. If possible, get a suite or two adjoining rooms, or rent or borrow a condo at a resort. The second room may only be used for your luggage, but it gives you a little breathing space and breaks up the deadly intimacy of a single hotel room. If you do opt for just one room, choose a hotel with large rooms and a sitting area. A large bathroom with counter space is certainly a plus. If you are a light sleeper, don't choose a hotel on a busy highway. Be sure there is air-conditioning or heating as the season requires.

Let him see you in a different light. Make this a romantic weekend. If you usually are the wholesome type, wear a sexy nightgown or a teddy. If you are usually sophisticated, be playful and girlish. If you are glamorous and sexy and he likes you that way, be *outrageously* glamorous and sexy. Order something from the Frederick's of Hollywood catalog. If you wear your hair down, put it up. If you wear it short, get a fancy comb or bow. In other words, be slightly different than usual. He'll be intrigued, and he will also try harder to please you because suddenly he will see a new side of you and subconsciously realize that he can't take you for granted. Men are usually delighted when their women do something to spice up the relationship. Believe it or not, most men are too unimaginative or shy to try these tricks, but they welcome a change.

Don't go somewhere that might make you uncomfortable on the first trip. If you get seasick, don't go on a weekend sailing trip. If neither of you have skied before, don't go skiing. If you hate the sun, don't try to be a good sport and spend a weekend at the beach. If you hate to drive, don't take a seven-hour car trip. If you're not the rustic type, don't go camping. In other words, do something that fits both your comfort zones. You want to minimize any situation that might cause complaints, stress, anxiety, danger, discomfort, or dissension.

The operative word here is *planning*. A first trip away with a man should be carefully planned and orchestrated to provide a relaxed and trouble-free atmosphere. If one of you likes to plan everything down to the minute and the other believes in total spontaneity, work it out in advance of your trip. You both may have to compromise, but don't compromise beyond the level of your own comfort zone. Otherwise, you'll be miserable.

Valerie went away with a man she had been seeing for about three months. He was charming, intellectual, and afflicted with terminal wanderlust. He hated making reservations or any advance plans. Valerie, whose usual nature is quite the opposite, thought this sounded carefree and romantic.

What she didn't bargain for was weekend traffic, holiday crowds, and a string of no vacancy signs. As darkness was falling and they still didn't have a room, all romantic dreams faded. They were irritated, hungry, and tired. Tempers flared, and the weekend rapidly disintegrated. They wound up in the servants' quarters of a small inn, with a squeaky Murphy bed, ancient nonfunctioning plumbing, and peeling wallpaper. Valerie tried to be a good sport, but this wasn't her idea of fun; she realized that this man, attractive though he was, would be all wrong for her in a permanent relationship. Although she had been charmed by his unstructured lifestyle, it took this weekend to make her accept the fact that they were simply incompatible in nature and outlook.

If your travel styles are at odds, you may find that the rest of your relationship soon will be. Sometimes opposites are good for each other, and a carefree, adventurous partner is a tonic for one who is usually a stick-in-the-mud. That's great if it feels good to you.

But as in Valerie's case, if the man's travel style
upsets your comfort zone and you have major conflicts, it is a good sign that the relationship will never
work.

You can tell a lot about a man when you travel
with him, and you should be careful to watch for
signs of real potential conflict. We don't mean the
normal irritability of a too-long flight or harsh words
to the desk clerk when your reservation isn't hon-
ored. We mean, for instance, how he does or doesn't
like to spend money. Do you like to stay at first class
hotels while he insists on staying at out-of-the way,
inexpensive inns? Are you an adventurous diner, and
he gets squeamish at anything stranger than lamb
chops? Do you splurge on cabs, and he insists on the
subway? Do you like to dance all night, and he likes
to turn in early so he can be up with the birds? Do
you like to watch the local scene at a quaint sidewalk
cafe, and he thinks that's a nonproductive waste of
time? Do you like to talk to strangers, and he doesn't?
If you have a travel emergency, does he handle it or
do you? If it's you, would you prefer it was him? Do
you feel strained and put upon, even though you're
trying to have fun?

Naturally, you can't agree on everything, and of
course you're two different people with different
natures and responses. But you should be mostly
compatible in matters that count to you. If he would
rather die than go shopping, and you hate art galleries, it's perfectly all right to split for the day so you
can do your thing and he can do his. But you should
be able to count on his rejoining you at an agreed
upon time. Or perhaps you can endure each other's
interests for the sake of getting to know each other
better. Major conflicts arise if you don't agree on
accommodations, expenditures, or travel style, or if

you feel he over- or underreacts to things. In other words, when you are away on a trip with a man, you should feel safe, protected, happy, and carefree. If you don't and too many conflicts arise, don't chalk them up to travel tension; realize that what you see is what you'll get when you are back home.

Travel usually magnifies the bad or accentuates the good. It's a microcosm of what living with him will be like. Before you commit your future to a man, we strongly advise you to take not one but several trips with him, even if it's only a weekend at a convention or your college homecoming. If you can get away together for at least a week, it will be a good investment and well worth the time and money.

11
Children:
Yours and His

If you have been married before there's a pretty good chance that you have one or more children. If they are living with you it may cause some difficulties in your relationship with your new man unless you take some precautionary steps. On one hand, you're ready to get on with your life and bring a new love into your home. On the other hand, the children who already live in your home are possibly going to be resentful—and ready to let their feelings show.

If your children are young, you have to deal with finding babysitters, guilt feelings about single parenting, last-minute cancellations of plans due to child-related emergencies, and the multitude of other responsibilities that come with the territory. If a man has not had children of his own, he very often doesn't understand the need to adjust your plans to accommodate car pools, unavailable babysitters, and the countless other last-minute situations that arise with children. (You can help the situation by keeping a list of reliable babysitters that you can call on short notice. You never know when you might meet someone wonderful who is so intrigued by you that he can't wait for more than a day or two to see you again.)

Like it or not, some men feel that children or teenagers around the house are an intrusion. If you see in the beginning that a man doesn't relate well to your children and seems uncomfortable in their presence, you had better have second thoughts about him. Of course, if you're a master of the Venus formula, you may be able to enchant him sufficiently to make up for *anything*, but you'll inevitably run into conflicts later on unless you are willing to make some major compromises.

One woman we interviewed did make a drastic decision in order to keep the man she wanted to marry. She had her teenage son move in with her parents because her husband-to-be didn't want children to complicate their lives and disrupt the traveling he enjoyed. They are still married after many years, but her relationship with her son is not close. She made a major sacrifice, and only she knows whether it was worth it.

SETTING AN EXAMPLE

In the case of teenage children, the problems become even more complex. As the relationship develops, you have to deal with whether to allow him to spend the night and how to explain it to the kids. Women seem to express two different schools of thought on the subject, but we conclude that it is better *not* to have a man spend the night when the kids are around, unless you have a committed relationship that is going to culminate in marriage. This may sound like old-fashioned advice, but most preteens and teenagers resent having their mother's boyfriend facing them across the breakfast table. It can be embarrassing for them to be confronted by their mother's sexuality, even though they know it exists. And you may be setting an example that can come back to haunt you later ("Oh, it's okay for *you* but not for me?").

The other side of the coin is that once your child is old enough to understand the situation (usually around ten years old), he or she should be told that Mom has to have her life, too, that she and Joe like each other a lot and enjoy spending the night together and that being together is a natural thing for mature adults who are thinking about living together permanently.

The risk is that if a relationship doesn't work out, your child may become suspicious and confused about your future relationships. Before Teddi remarried, she was dating steadily a man who she thought she might marry. Her daughter was about ten years old at the time, and she was uncomfortable at first with this man's presence. However, the man had a child of the same age, and after a while it became natural for all of them to be together on weekends. When things didn't work out and they broke up after a year, Teddi's daughter was definitely wary of the next man in her mother's life. Happily, the new relationship *did* work out, and that man is now Teddi's husband.

In the long run, it's probably a better idea to stay at the man's place, have the kids stay with friends, or go away for occasional weekends if you can work out the logistics. It's not a hard-and-fast rule, but it does eliminate some of the tensions that arise with your kids when there is a new man in the picture, and you want to be as considerate as possible of your children's feelings.

There are a number of other obstacles that you may encounter involving your children and the man you are hoping to marry. Some of them can be handled smoothly by using common sense and good communication techniques. Others are virtually insurmountable, and you will probably be wasting valuable time and effort if you try to fight the inevitable. Of course, there are always exceptions to the rule.

WHEN THE KIDS DON'T LIKE HIM

Let's start with the situations that can be handled. It is very common for a child, or even a teenager, to resent the new man in your life, especially one you are serious about. Kids can be pretty obnoxious, rude, incommunicative, and hostile when they set their minds to it, and this type of atmosphere does not make a man want to become part of your family. If you see your child reacting negatively to the man you are involved with, there are two positive steps you can take. First, sit down with your kids and have a warm, heart-to-heart conversation (this is not something you should scream about—it will only guarantee that they'll dislike the man even more). Explain that this man is a very special friend, just like *they* have special friends. Point out that you'd never be rude or mean to their friends, and they should be able to show the same courtesy to yours. Keep in mind that it's probably very difficult for them to see a new man come into their mother's life, possibly "replacing" their father, so give it time, and be sympathetic to their feelings.

The second thing you can do, particularly if your children make it clear that they have no intention of welcoming this man into their home, is to keep a safe distance between them and your man until you have a solid foundation for your new relationship. At that point, if you think he'll be understanding about it, explain to him your predicament and enlist his help in smoothing out the situation.

If you're fortunate and your children are more neutral about the relationship (and if your man is willing), plan an occasional family outing—maybe a movie and dinner, or a backyard cook-out at home. It's a great opportunity for everyone to get acquainted, and it will make the kids feel more involved in the relationship. If all goes well, they'll start to view him as someone other than the man who keeps taking Mom out of the house every night while they get stuck at home with the sitter.

DEALING WITH HIS KIDS

Aside from *your* children, you're also going to have to deal with his. It's very possible that his kids are going to be hostile to you, no matter how nice and charming you are. This can really devastate a relationship, but you can avoid a disaster if you use a little common sense and do your very best to make the children like you—especially if the man is very close to them.

Most women we've talked to agree that there are basically two types of single fathers. The first is completely engrossed with his kids and is determined to be a major influence in their lives, even if they aren't living in the same house. These men put their kids before a relationship with any woman. They won't break a date with their kids even if it means *you* staying home alone on your birthday. Daddy is always there for them even though it may mean he's *not* there for you. If the man you want falls into this category, it is important that his kids like you. If they do, half the battle is won. If they don't like you and set out to sabotage the relationship, they are likely to succeed. We know of one situation where the man's two adult children (both in their twenties) put so much pressure on him to attempt a reconciliation with their mother that he left the woman he planned to marry and moved back with his ex-wife to give it a try. It didn't work, and the ordeal ended his new relationship as well.

There are just as many men in the second category. These men are responsible fathers, pay their child support, and see their children on a regular basis, but aren't involved to the extent that it would affect their relationship with a woman. If your man fits this description, it still doesn't hurt to use a little charm on the kids—after all, you're thinking about marrying their father. What you *shouldn't* do is try to replace their mother in any way—and that includes offering unasked-for advice or doling out discipline. That is their parents' job, not yours.

We know a woman in her fifties whose second marriage was to a very successful, wealthy widower. He had a nineteen-year-old daughter who was a spoiled, selfish brat, and our friend was determined to straighten out the girl. She tried everything, from reasoning with her to yelling at her to setting up appointments (that were never kept) with psychologists. She also tried to convince her husband that he should lay down the law with his daughter. It soon became a three-way combat zone and the marriage broke up.

THINGS TO BE WARY OF

1. Don't always dismiss your children's instincts when it comes to judging the character of the man in your life. If your child is basically well-adjusted, nonmanipulative, accepting, and loving, and yet he or she has strong negative vibes about the man and actively dislikes him, listen to the reasons and weigh them carefully. Put your antennae out; the child may sense something you overlooked in the first flush of love.

2. If a man tells you right up front that he doesn't want to raise another set of kids, don't assume you can change his mind. There are many men who have spent years anticipating the freedom and reduced responsibility of having their kids grown and out on their own, and they are not willing to give that up for anyone. One man we interviewed talked of his last relationship to a woman with two small children. He told her up front that it could never lead to marriage because he had already raised three kids; he didn't want any more. But after eight months, during which they fell madly in love, she was sure she could change his mind. She was wrong. He did love her, but not enough to take on the responsibility of two kids for ten to fifteen years. He eventually ended the relationship.

3. There is a subtle sexuality that exudes from female teenagers. Don't subject the man you want to marry, or *any* man you date, to any even *unconscious* temptations in this area. Teenage girls who innocently walk around the house in skimpy clothes or underwear should be discouraged when

your man is around. Also, don't encourage lots of hugging and cuddling and kissing; this man is not her father.

4. Even adult children can throw a wrench into a relationship, but they are much easier to handle than children who live at home. There are times when a man's grown children don't want him to remarry for one reason or another (often financial), but generally, that type of interference can be overcome. If the man is truly committed to you, he won't let his grown children, who most likely have their own lives and families, stand in the way for long (unless he's a wimp!). But beware: men have been known to use those family objections to stall marriage and keep the status quo. Don't fall for that one.

To sum up, before you decide you are ready to remarry, come to terms with what you owe your children and what you owe yourself. You owe your children a harmonious environment in which they are loved and accepted, not just tolerated. You owe them a stepfather who may not become a substitute father, but at least doesn't resent them and make them feel like intruders. What you don't owe your children is the right to own you until they are ready to cut the apron strings and get on with their own lives. You don't owe them *your* chance for happiness and a new life, even if it means disrupting their lives by moving to another city. Children are very resilient, and they adjust.

Don't make the same mistake as a friend of ours from the South. Her husband left her after twenty-one years, and she was devastated. About a year after the divorce, she went on a cruise and met a wonderful man who lived in the East. They had a long-distance romance for about six months, but finally he wanted her to marry him and move her two teenagers to his city. She was blissfully happy and very much in love with him. However, when she broke the news to her kids and told them that they would be moving, they became hysterical. They were involved in school activities, their friends were all there, they'd kill themselves if they had to move, the whole works. She agonized over the situation for a few months and finally gave in to them. That was ten years ago. Today the kids are both married and living in other cities. She is alone.

The moral of this true story is: give your children all the love and support that you can, but remember, you count too!

12
The Fixer Upper

In California real estate parlance, a fixer upper is a house that has the basic qualities you want, but needs renovation and imagination to become your dream house.

A male fixer upper is a decent, kind, generous, ordinary-looking guy who has a lot of wonderful qualities and is crazy about you. You think he is a fine person, but . . . he's overweight, he has bad teeth, his glasses keep slipping down his nose, his clothes look like rejects from the local thrift shop, he says *you know* after every sentence, he still wears his hair in a pompadour, and you can't stand his cologne.

On the plus side, he is warm; giving; witty; good to his mother, ex-wife, and children; stable; and self-supporting—and he thinks you're wonderful.

If only you could get turned on by this guy, you *know* he would be a good companion and lots of fun—maybe even a terrific lover and husband. So

177

why not take him in hand and make him over?

As we have discussed earlier, you can't change a man's basic nature and personality. But there *are* subtle suggestions and compromises you can make to gently extract a few changes. Remember, there is a shortage of *all* types of men out there—let alone perfect ones. And let's face it, unless you are practically perfect yourself (how many of us are?), it may be tough to snag one of that endangered species. If you're holding out for the guy who already has a combination of chiseled features, thick wavy hair, perfect teeth, gorgeous physique, impeccably tailored clothes, and natural athletic ability, as well as being socially prominent, witty, kind, generous, sensitive, tender, a fabulous lover, a brilliant conversationalist, and completely enthralled with only *you;* you may be spending many nights alone. But don't declare defeat yet! The man you decide on may not be any or all of those things when you meet him, but he hasn't yet been the object of your gentle guidance and power of the Venus formula!

LOOKING BEYOND THE PHYSICAL

If you learn to look beyond that first impression and mentally strip away exterior flaws, you may find the makings of your dream man underneath it all. Don't forget, we women have been forced to take many more pains with our appearance, personality, and general persona than have men. Throughout the ages, women have sought out ways to enhance their image for men. Men have made their impact through their strength, their brains and their material successes rather than through physical allurement. Of course, handsome men are admired by women, but we have yet to meet a woman who ranks movie-star looks anywhere near the top of her list of requirements in a man. We do, however, put stock in the wrappings, such as taste in clothes, hair styles, grooming, social skills, mannerisms, and the like. Whether or not they admit it, most men want these attributes but may not know how to go about attaining them. You would be surprised how many princes there are just waiting to shed their froggy exteriors and be led, ever so subtly, to a whole new image by a special woman.

Take the example of our friend Kate. After a bitter divorce and six years of looking unsuccessfully for a satisfying new relationship (which to her meant marriage), she took stock of the men she had dated and tried to analyze why nothing had worked. She realized that she had only been attracted to handsome, sophisticated, socially active, big shot types like her former husband, who took her to expensive restaurants and lots of parties, and who had extremely outgoing personalities. After a few weeks they invariably dropped Kate and moved on to someone younger, or prettier, or more exciting, or just plain new. This type of man has his pick of practically any woman he wants, likes variety, and is generally not the type to settle down and make a commitment to one woman. Sure, these supercharmers are glamorous and exciting, but if you're looking for the long haul, they're not a good bet!

But Kate is basically a smart, intuitive woman, and she realized she was in a negative and destructive pattern. So, she decided to stop dating completely for a few months until she figured out a new plan of action. She stuck to her guns and didn't go out with anyone except a long-time platonic friend, Phil, who often took her two sons to ball games while she was out with one of her dates.

Phil, a dentist, weighed twenty pounds too much,

was going bald, wore Hawaiian shirts, and preferred hot dogs and baseball with the kids to fancy parties and elegant restaurants. Although Kate didn't care a hoot for baseball or hot dogs, she began to accompany Phil and the boys on the weekends when she wasn't attending the theatre or a ballet, both of which she loved. Before long, Phil was spending evenings during the week at the house. They would play chess—the three of them patiently teaching Kate— and sometimes Phil would cook a gourmet dinner.

Inevitably, Kate and Phil got to know each other, and Kate liked what she found. She learned that Phil was understanding and perceptive, and had a zany sense of humor and a wonderful gentleness underneath his somewhat gruff exterior. She also discovered, to her surprise, that one evening when he massaged a kink out of her shoulders, she felt some sexual stirrings.

It was at that point that Kate took a good, hard look at Phil. She had suspected for some time that he was attracted to her, and she began to analyze her own feelings. She acknowledged that she didn't feel the earth moving or hear bells chiming with Phil, but she did respect him as human being, enjoy his company, and truly *like* him. She also realized that he had potential to become even more appealing to her.

To make a long story short, Kate presented Phil with a gift certificate to her health club on Valentine's Day, along with a beautiful velour warm-up suit and told him how much fun it would be for her to have someone with whom she could work out. She bemoaned the fact that she was having trouble sticking to a healthy diet alone—the boys were no help— and asked Phil to help her out by sharing her diet meals. (Kate was slim and trim and not a pound overweight). The relationship progressed. Before long, Phil realized to his delight that Kate was beginning to care about him in a different way.

Within two months, Kate engineered a shopping trip to rehabilitate Phil's wardrobe (complimenting him on how handsome he looked in the new clothes), accompanied him to a new hair stylist for a more flattering haircut, and persuaded him to join her for his first experience at the ballet and a late super afterward. He was pleasantly surprised at how much he enjoyed the evening. And guess what? Just as in Pygmalion, Kate fell in love with her creation. They have now been married for more than two years. Phil still prefers baseball to ballet, but he is fifteen pounds lighter, sports a trim mustache and beard (you hardly notice his thinning hair) and, although he still wears an occasional Hawaiian shirt around the house, has a closet filled with smart clothes, lovingly selected by Kate.

Ronda had an even greater challenge with George. After two unhappy marriages and a succession of blind dates that didn't work, a friend introduced her to George. They were totally different in nature: he was painfully shy, unsophisticated, and reserved; she was worldly, outgoing, and vivacious. Both were average looking. But George was so taken with Ronda's charm and sparkle that he willingly accompanied her to parties, the theater, anything and everything she wanted. The problem was that George's personality, past experiences, and personal style didn't fit Ronda's vision of the right man—but there was something about him that truly attracted her. Although he was the owner of a successful business and could afford the kind of life that Ronda wanted, he just didn't feel comfortable with it. Still, he loved Ronda and wanted

to make her happy. Ronda had already gone the pas-
sionate-love-at-first-sight route with her two former
husbands, and she was smart enough to realize that
the deep affection she felt for George had much more
staying power. So she began a subtle campaign to
smooth out George's rough edges.

First, she picked an area in which George was
comfortable and knowledgeable. It happened to be
jazz. She began inviting people who shared that interest to small dinner parties featuring local musicians.
Of course, George was the expert, and he began to
enjoy the role. He also was an avid history buff, and
Ronda gradually coaxed him to share his knowledge
in that area also. It wasn't long before he felt comfortable and relaxed at the social gatherings that Ronda
loved. Her praise and pride at the way he had blos-
somed were all the incentive he needed.

Within a year, Ronda had persuaded George to join
a country club (he was a good golfer but had always
played alone) and refurbish his somewhat old-fashioned wardrobe. By the time Ronda and George were
married, he was so delighted with his new image—
inside and out—that he insisted on a big reception
instead of the small, quiet affair they had discussed.
It turned out to be the best party either one of them
ever attended.

Kate's and Ronda's happy endings didn't come by
accident, and there were plenty of rough spots and
setbacks along the way. Remaking a man to fit your
dreams takes determination, subtle manipulation,
praise, and above all, patience.

RECOGNIZING A FIXER UPPER

This can be tricky. Sometimes what you see on the
surface is *all* there is.

There are four basic requirements:

1. First of all, he should already want you. It is much easier to change a man if he is doing it for someone he's crazy about. You may not have been using the full impact of the Venus formula with him because you hadn't thought of him as a possible mate, but it's an important step to make before you begin working on the transformation.

2. His financial prospects should be somewhere in the range that you want. Generally, by the age of thirty-five or so, a man has established his income potential and pattern. If you're looking at a man who considers twenty thousand a year enough to live on comfortably and happily, you will have a tough time changing him into someone who regularly vacations in Europe and considers Jaguars to be a standard necessity of life. Needless to say, a man who has trouble keeping a job and earning a living is rarely going to become a good provider or an ambitious achiever. There are certain character flaws that no woman can correct.

3. He should have a flexible nature. Beware of the man who has to eat at the same time every night, won't try anything new, must get up and out of bed early, even on weekends, and never varies from his routine. If a man is really cemented into his ways, he won't be able to change even if he wants to.

4. He must be basically kind, good-natured, anxious to please you, generous of spirit (and wallet, to the extent he can afford), and honest—someone you respect as a human being.

Take inventory of the men you know—the ones

you have never considered as prospects. Maybe there's someone you work with every day but really don't see, maybe because he has acne, or dandruff, or wears polyester suits. Or it could be the nice but plain accountant who is so wonderful about helping with your taxes but refuses to let you pay a cent. Or maybe it's good old Joe, who is always available when you need a last-minute escort or someone to take your dog to the vet or check out your car battery, but who has a Brooklyn accent and frizzy hair and never wears anything that matches. Or it could be Jim, who would have been great if he didn't stutter and were more exciting in bed. You can probably come up with dozens of men you haven't given a second thought to because they didn't fit your preconceived notions of the right man.

Remember the analogy of the house that has the basics but needs imagination and refurbishing. Think of all the possibilities available to restore a house: painting, papering, reconstructing, refinishing, polishing, rearranging. There are just as many means available to fix up a human being. After all, women think nothing of using every available method to camouflage and improve themselves. In addition to the obvious, such as wardrobe, physical fitness, and corrective dentistry, there is speech therapy, hair transplants or hairpieces, lessons in tennis, golf, or any other sport, skin treatments, etiquette lessons, sex therapy, courses in culture and the arts, contact lenses—even plastic surgery. No one wants to be told that they need a major overhaul; the process must be handled very delicately and tactfully. But when a man sees admiration reflected in the eyes of the woman he loves, it is a powerful incentive to be whatever she wants him to be.

Sometimes it takes a near-catastrophe to show us that there are alternate paths to happiness and to give us the insight to follow them. That was the case with Joanne. After her husband left her, she spent four unhappy years trying to find someone who could fill his shoes. He was a tough act to follow. Tall, handsome, wealthy, charming, but unfortunately, not faithful. After several love affairs, he had left her for another woman.

A friend fixed Joanne up with a blind date. When Al arrived, she was careful to hide her disappointment. He was shorter than she, had a paunch and bad teeth, and wore unflattering, rimless glasses. However, the evening wasn't as bad as she expected. Al was an articulate and amusing conversationalist and she found herself thoroughly enjoying his company. They continued to date, and although he was falling more and more in love, she thought of him as just a good friend. Then she had a near-fatal auto accident and was incapacitated for over two months. The devotion, nurturing, and love that she received from Al during that time gave her the insight to see beyond his less-than-perfect exterior, and realize that the interior was pure gold. The exterior she could take care of later—which she did. Today, Al is still three inches shorter than Joanne (but so what?), his paunch is gone, thanks to Joanne's creative suggestion that they make love after jogging as a reward to them both for keeping in shape. He now wears contact lenses and is often complimented about his beautiful teeth—now capped, a wedding present from Joanne.

If you find a man who has the basic qualities—who is beautiful inside—the right woman can make the outside match the inside. But remember, it takes real caring, tons of reinforcement, praise, gentle encour-agement, and the foresight to visualize the finished product.

There is an added bonus to successfully remaking a fixer upper. He will be so happy about the finished product, so delighted with his new image, and so grateful to the wonderful woman who inspired it, that he will love you even more than he thought possible. And even if he didn't *start out* as the man of your dreams, you may find that your Prince Charm-ing did indeed arrive—in disguise at first, but now there for all the world to see.

13
Trade-Offs or Necessary Choices

There may come a time in your life when you must make some serious decisions about your future. You may have been through a bad marriage or a number of dead-end romances, you may be a baby boomer facing the possibility that your biological clock is running out, you may be on the brink of financial disaster, you may be getting older and realizing that the ratio of men to women is not working in your favor, or you may just be tired of the chase, ready to declare permanent celibacy and write men out of your life completely.

Let's face it, none of us likes to acknowledge, even to ourselves, that we may not be able to realize all of the hopes and dreams that we have harbored since childhood. We tend to hang on to those dreams far beyond the time it is likely we will achieve them. This is particularly true when it comes to looking for the right man. We all start out dreaming of a perfect someone who is tall, handsome, rich, witty, and brilliant, and maybe your first husband *was* your ideal man. But now that you're single again, let's be practical. If it is really important for you to find a permanent relationship and settle down with one man again, and yet you haven't been able to make that happen, maybe it's time to sit down and take a good hard look at what you're aiming for and how realistic your chances are for attracting the kind of man you want. There may be a terrific guy out there who could make you very happy but who may not fit your preconceived notions about what the ideal man should be.

Take the example of Laura. Divorced at thirty-four, she was very anxious to remarry and start a family. She is a partner in a major law firm, and like many women of her generation, she had devoted her time and efforts to developing her career rather than starting a family. When it finally dawned on her that her childbearing years were running out, she decided it was time to get serious about marriage. She also realized that most of the eligible men in her age bracket were already taken, and most of the men she had been dating were older, divorced, already had children, and had no desire to start new families. She had always been attracted to tall, athletic, outgoing, ambitious men who equaled her in looks, education, and earning ability (she had plenty of all three). The older men she dated fit the bill perfectly and she was never lacking some kind of romance in her life.

When it came to commitment and marriage, however, it was another story. Every man she met whom she considered qualified seemed to be either a playboy, married, gay, emotionally damaged, or not ready for commitment. Meanwhile, the clock kept ticking.

After a year of searching, she was so discouraged that Paul, one of the young associates in her firm, noticed she seemed depressed and asked her what was wrong. He was around her age, shorter than she, somewhat scrawny, and not particularly attractive—certainly not the type that she would ever look at twice. He asked her to lunch, and he seemed so sincere and concerned that she went. Over lunch she found out that he was single, that he didn't have many friends because he was very shy, and that he had very little experience with women.

Laura felt comfortable with him because he seemed genuinely kind and interested in her. She certainly didn't feel any sexual sparks. He began asking her to lunch on a regular basis, and then it became dinner a couple of times a week. During this period, Laura continued her search for the right man to marry, all the while becoming more and more discouraged. The only person she could count on to always be there for her, cheer her up, make her laugh, encourage her, and accept her faults was—you guessed it—Paul.

One morning, Laura woke up and realized she was thirty-six. A dozen roses from Paul were delivered wishing her a happy birthday. That night he took her out for a special dinner at her favorite restaurant. Over coffee he told her he wanted to marry her. She wasn't surprised—she had sensed he was falling in love with her. She also knew she wasn't in love with him. She loved him as a person, and she admired him as a human being. They had kissed a few times but that was the extent of their physical relationship. She wasn't electrified by the contact, but she wasn't repulsed either. In fact, she was surprised at the emotional intensity and passion he exhibited when they were kissing. She told him she would think about his proposal and let him know in a week.

That night, she mentally calculated Paul's positives and negatives. On the negative side, he was not as ambitious as she. He didn't earn nearly as much money. He wasn't good-looking. He faded into the walls when he was with a group. He wasn't dynamic. He didn't ring bells for her sexually.

On the positive side, he was dependable, honest, kind, warm, had a good sense of humor, loved children, had a stable profession, and showed signs of being a good lover.

She also evaluated her own situation. She wanted to get married. She wanted to have children. She had spent two years looking for the ideal man with no success. The ratio of eligible men was decreasing, and she truly enjoyed Paul's company. She decided to give it a try.

They got engaged. They have now been married for six years and have twins, with another baby on the way. Laura is still a successful attorney and still makes more money than Paul, who is comfortable with the lower pressure level of an associate with the firm. She has what she wanted: a career, a family, and a man who adores her. She may not be passionately aflame with insatiable love, but she is happy and fulfilled. So is he.

The moral of this story is that those feelings we associate with love—excitement, sexual longing, breathless anticipation, intense jealousy, constant yearning and craving—are not always necessary for a good marriage. Sure, it's great to have rockets exploding and flutterings in your tummy but they don't always provide the long-term foundation for a solid relationship.

ARE YOU REACHING TOO HIGH?

There are certain qualities that most women seek in their ideal potential mate, qualities that are usually based on fantasy rather than reality. If you find that these traits are high on your list of priorities, you may have a hard time finding the right man.

Romantic Gestures

Gestures such as sending flowers and gifts and saying "I love you" regularly are nice, but not necessary. It is great to have a man who will do these things, but there are plenty of very nice guys whose minds just don't work that way. It's not that they are cold or mean or uncaring—it's just not their nature. Your best tactic with this type of man is to set the example for him. As your relationship develops, do the things for him that you would like him to do for you. But don't criticize him and don't complain about the things he doesn't do. Eventually, he'll probably get the message. But even if he doesn't, if he has other good qualities, just keep in mind that you're not perfect, either.

An Aura of Passion and Excitement

Exciting men are wonderful, and we all would like excitement in our relationships. But how long do you think that initial adrenaline rush is going to last? Even the most passionate love develops into a comfortable, steady glow after a few years. In fact, if the decibels are too high in the beginning, the natural tapering off can be too great an adjustment for the relationship to survive.

If you want excitement in your life, make it *your* responsibility to generate it. There are dozens of books on how to spice up your sex life and stimulate passion in a man. There are plenty of surprises you can cook up to bring excitement into your life—just use your imagination.

Complete Openness and Emotional Self-Disclosure

The "me" generation set the trend toward "letting it all hang out" and promoted the idea that in order to have a good relationship, two people must bare their souls to each other and share every fear, anxiety, character flaw, and weakness. That just doesn't work for some people, especially men, who are not conditioned to express their feelings freely.

Of course, you must be able to communicate with your mate, but if you have a man who tends to keep a lot of his feelings and problems to himself, don't write him off for that reason alone. Usually, as this type of man feels more comfortable and safe with you (and with your gentle encouragement), he will share more of himself. He may never become an open book but, remember, a good man is a lot harder to find than a good book!

Immediate Physical Attraction

Every woman dreams of looking across a crowded room, locking eyes with a stranger, and feeling the earth tremble. This does happen occasionally (especially if you live in earthquake zones), but most long-term relationships don't start that way. As a matter of fact, almost every love affair we found that *did* start that way didn't last. One of the biggest mistakes a woman can make is underestimating the value of a man just because he doesn't initially turn her on. Literally hundreds of women with whom we spoke while researching this book told us they were not sexually attracted to their husbands when they first met them. Sexual compatibility can develop as a relationship progresses. Unfortunately, a lot of men don't understand this and won't bother to get to know a woman if that instant chemistry isn't there—and they miss out on some terrific women because of this. Women, because of the numbers, can't afford to make that mistake. Some of the best men come on slow—and they are worth the wait.

Ann has just married Ben, a man she was not even interested in dating when she first met him. They were introduced at a sales meeting, and she didn't give him a second glance. He was the complete opposite of any man she had ever been attracted to—a little overweight, balding, and slightly frumpy in his tweed suit. During the three-day sales meeting, they found themselves in the same workshop groups, and along with a few others, drifted out together for lunches and dinners. Ann discovered that they lived in the same neighborhood and both had eight-year-old sons. She also noticed that he had an offbeat, acerbic wit very much like her own. By the end of the sales meeting, they had become buddies and decided to get together with their kids for a Sunday picnic and an early movie. Everyone had such a good time that they decided to go out together again the following week. That was followed by dinner at Ann's house with the two of them cooking while the kids played video games. Ann was delighted to have a male friend with whom she could have fun and include her son. She still wasn't thinking about romance because, after all, when that special spark is there you know it right away. Right? Wrong! After a few months of wonderful times spent with her new "extended family," it dawned on Ann that she was enjoying her time with Ben more than she had enjoyed anyone's company in a long time.

One evening after dinner, they were sitting on the

couch having a brandy when right in the middle of a sentence they looked at each other and—whammy—it happened. They kissed and those bells rang—after three months. Ann said she will be eternally grateful to her son because she would never have even gone out with Ben if it weren't a family outing.

Someone You Think Will Impress Your Friends

Most of us are guilty of putting too much stock in what our friends think of our choice of men. Consciously or unconsciously, we want our friends to be a little envious of the man in our life. We don't want to hear whispers of "What does she see in him?", or "I wouldn't go out with that creep," or "She can certainly do better than that!"

If you do have "friends" who insist on making such remarks, take them with a grain of salt. There are women who find flaws in any man who isn't interested in *them*. If you will find a man with whom you are compatible and happy, but your friends make fun of him or put him down for whatever reason, they aren't your friends. (Unless, of course, he is an ex-con, cat burglar, embezzler, or Bluebeard and you aren't aware of it.)

A certain snobbism still exists with some women when it comes to men who work with their hands rather than in an office, even though many blue collar workers earn more than a lot of white collar ones. You can pass up some fabulous men if you have that prejudice. We know someone who did.

Glenda met Rudy, an electrician, at a church party and they spent most of the evening dancing and talking. He wasn't traditionally good-looking, but she found him warm, lovable, and genuinely nice, and she accepted a date with him for the next evening. That evening led to another date and another. Glenda was becoming more and more involved with Rudy. One thing concerned her, though: the fact that he was an electrician and not the professional man she had always envisioned herself marrying. In fact, it bothered her so much that she told her friends that he was an "electrical contractor."

One of Glenda's friends was having a cocktail party, and she invited Glenda and Rudy. It would be the first time Rudy would meet Glenda's group, and she realized her little deception about his work would be discovered. So she compounded her mistake and added insult to injury by asking Rudy if he would mind saying he was an electrical contractor because this group would relate to him better if he did. He told her in no uncertain terms that he was proud of who and what he was and although he had thought he was in love with her, he had clearly made a big mistake in his appraisal of her values and his perception of the kind of person she was. Realizing she had been an idiot, she called him to apologize and asked if they could try again; but the bond was broken, and their romance just fizzled out. She still regrets her elitist attitude and hasn't yet met anyone she cares for in the same way.

We don't mean to say you shouldn't seek someone of your own class and status with whom to spend your life. Generally, the more two people have in common, the easier and more compatible the relationship. However, remember that there are some wonderful guys who may not wear three-piece suits to work but who are kind, loving, sexy, dependable, and available. So think long and hard about your priorities.

WHAT DO YOU REALLY WANT

The idea of coming down a notch or two in your expectations for a marriage partner may be hard for you to accept, especially if you are exceptionally young and attractive, or if your former husband was a class act in ways that mattered to you. In making that decision, consider your age, appearance, financial status, lifestyle, past successes with men, and how long you have been single. These are all elements that should determine just how realistic your expectations are.

If you have made the most of all your attributes and still haven't attracted the man you want, then it is time to sit down and reevaluate. Write down a detailed description of the type of man you have been trying to attract. List his emotional characteristics as well as his obvious ones. We asked one of our research subjects to do this—here's her list:

1. Financially secure—upper income strata.

2. Professional or businessman.

3. Taller than I am.

4. Not more than ten pounds overweight.

5. Intellectually superior to me.

6. Likes tennis and horseback riding.

7. Hates football.

8. Outgoing and articulate.

9. Great lover.

10. Sensitive and emotional.

11. Affectionate.

12. Stable and reliable.

13. Good sense of humor—funny.

14. Loves to buy me surprises.

15. Not fussy about food.

16. Flexible and easygoing.

17. Compassionate and understanding.

18. Popular with others.

19. Admired at work.

20. Desirable to other women.

21. Likes to travel.

22. Likes my kids.

Quite a tough bill to fill! Our friend has been searching for eight years with no luck. This woman is charming and attractive, and has an appealing aura about her. Men are attracted to her and she dates a lot, but she never seems to find the kind of man she has been looking for. She has had a few long-term relationships that ended because the men fell short of her expectations, and she didn't really put much energy into making them work. She told us she was tired of being alone, sick of dating, and more than ready to settle down into a traditional relationship, which to her meant marriage. But after eight years she had just about given up hope of ever finding someone.

We suggested she rethink her priorities and make another list. This time we asked her to leave out qualities on the first list that she would be willing to give up if, in return, she would have a husband who fulfilled at least 50 percent of her *needs*, not *desires*. Here's what was left:

1. Financially equal to her.

2. Sensitive.

3. Affectionate.

4. Stable and reliable

5. Good sense of humor.

6. Compassionate and understanding.

7. Likes my kids.

8. Enjoys sex.

9. Loves me and wants to get married.

Why should you compromise so much when it comes to the person you hope to spend the rest of your life with? Well, you shouldn't, if you're lucky enough to find everything you want in one man. The trouble is that there are so few men who fit into that perfect ten category, and unless *you* are a perfect ten yourself, or happen to fit a man's particular fantasy, the odds are not good that you will end up with one. That doesn't mean you can't find a wonderful guy and have him by your side forever. He may not be the romance novel's stereotypic dream man, but if you play your cards right, you may wind up with a bigger jackpot than you expected.

MARRYING FOR "OTHER REASONS"

There is another trade-off in the mating game that happens all the time, but no one likes to admit they have made it: finding a man who is less than what you have dreamed about but who can offer you a greatly improved lifestyle. For one reason or another, a woman can find herself facing overwhelming financial and emotional stress. Maybe despite her best efforts, circumstances make it impossible to get her life going in the direction in which she had hoped and planned. This may be the time for her to consider setting out to find a man who will help her shoulder her burdens. It may not be her first choice, but we believe in facing reality, even when it doesn't coincide with current popular attitudes.

You may be saying, wouldn't women with any self-respect become bag ladies before they would even consider anything so *dishonest*? Well, before you stone and quarter us for such an outrageous suggestion, remember that there are situations where this type of trade-off may be the only sensible answer; and then think about the benefits received by the man on the other end of the bargain. This is certainly not a new concept. Throughout history there have been marriages of convenience that have developed into lifelong, deep affection. Love has never been the *only* reason for marriage. She may grow to love the man, or it may not last forever, but if she plays the game fairly, he will get as much out of the deal as she does. In return for saving her from financial or emotional disaster, he is entitled to her respect, kindness, consideration, best sexual efforts, and all of the special magic she has to offer. If she's smart, she certainly isn't going to tell him that she's "settling" for him— she'll make him feel as if he is the man of her dreams.

We met a woman who decided to rethink her taste in men after two failed marriages and about a dozen dead-end relationships with the type of men to whom she had always been attracted—good looking, party-loving, muscular, flashy, big spenders, who were highly sexed, highly egotistical, and unfortunately, very unreliable.

One day she was reluctantly fixed up with a stock-broker whose idea of a good time was a quiet dinner for two followed by an evening at the symphony and home to bed by 11:00 P.M. because he had to be up at 5:00 A.M. He was nondescript in appearance, shy, and not very sophisticated sexually. But he was totally fascinated by her and thought everything she did was adorable and wonderful. He also called when he said he would, treated her with the kind of old-fashioned chivalry that women love (even if they won't admit it), and let her know that he would always be there when she needed him. They were married six months after they met.

No, she didn't fall madly in love with him. Yes, she is occasionally bored with him. No, he didn't become a perfect lover. Yes, she does miss some parties be-cause he has to get up early, and yes, she occasionally longs for the excitement of those other guys. Does she regret her decision? Not for a minute. What she got instead of roller-coaster highs (and devastating lows), late night discos, and the surface glitter of a playboy's charm, was a kind and loving man who is totally devoted to her. What he got is a woman who is shrewd enough to know when she's ahead and uses all principles of the Venus formula to make sure he never forgets how lucky he is.

HOW TO BEND AND NOT BREAK

There is another type of trade-off that is a little less controversial. Actually, most women wind up mak-ing this accommodation to some extent with the men in their lives. What it amounts to is giving in to certain needs your man has, even though it may be something you feel is silly, childish, or unreasonable. We *do not* advocate doing anything for a man (or *anyone* for that matter) that goes against your moral standards, reduces your self-esteem, or compromises your principles. What we're talking about is doing something you might not otherwise do, simply because it is important to your man. This goes beyond compromise; it mean sacrificing your own desires in certain areas in order to get what you want in the long run. Of course, the end must justify the means.

It did for Coreen. She was in love with Fritz, who was as close to her dream man as anyone could hope to find. He had all the qualities she wanted in a man. Unfortunately, he made a few demands she didn't care for. He insisted she join him when he was ready to go to sleep. He wanted her to be right there next to him, with the TV and the lights off, at his bedtime, which was normally 10:00 P.M. Coreen had always been something of a night owl, and for the six months they had been together this had been a bone of contention in their relationship. Fritz also loved getting up at 6:00 A.M. having breakfast with Coreen, reading the paper together, and discussing the headlines over their coffee before they went to work. Coreen, on the other hand, is the type who doesn't want to be spoken to until after her second cup of coffee, preferably not until at least 9:30 A.M.

Of course, it seems totally unreasonable that Fritz would expect Coreen to change her lifetime habits on his account. She asked herself why she should agree to something as nonsensical as turning out the lights just because *he* was ready to go to sleep, or chatting about the news when all she really wants is to listen to the "Today" show alone. If Fritz really loved her, how could he expect her to bend to his will regardless of her wishes?

She decided it was true that Fritz was unreasonable in his demands. But she also acknowledged she had never met a man who was so perfect for her in every other way. In fact, most of the men she had known were unreasonable in one way or another, but none of them met as many of her needs as Fritz did. That extra hour of reading and watching the late show was enjoyable, but was it really *that* important in her life? She decided it wasn't nearly as important as Fritz. As for the early morning tête-â-têtes, she told him she would go along as cheerfully as possible during the week, if on weekends he would either sleep in with her or breakfast alone. He thought that was fair. Coreen still looks forward to those weekends and sometimes sneaks into the den for a late movie after Fritz is asleep. But they have been happily married for fifteen years.

THE TAKE IT OR LEAVE IT SITUATION

Another type of trade-off many women face is having to either accept a difficult situation or lose the man. This happened to Carol.

When Carol started dating Howard, she knew he lived with his eighty-year-old father. Howard had had a very close and loving relationship with his parents, and when his mother died, he took his father to live with his wife and him. Then his wife died, leaving Howard and his father in the house.

Unlike Howard, who was easygoing, charming, warm, and very lovable, his father was not a very pleasant man. He resented Carol, and was generally grumpy and uncommunicative in her presence. This was annoying to her but not a major problem, since she didn't spend that much time in his company.

When Howard proposed, she was very happy, but she also faced a dilemma. The prospect of living in the same house with her father-in-law was more than she felt she could handle.

She explained to Howard that she loved him very much but that she wouldn't be happy under the same roof with his father. Howard admitted that his father was difficult but made it very clear that he intended to share his home with him for as long as his father lived. Carol knew that Howard had been married for many years and that he felt more comfortable in a traditional lifestyle. She sensed that the time was right for him for marriage and that if it didn't happen, they would gradually drift apart and he would most likely meet and marry someone else. She evaluated Howard's good qualities and the fact that she truly loved him, and measured this against the day-to-day reality of having his father around all the time. She decided that spending the rest of her life with a man who loved her and whom she loved was a fair trade for putting up with an old man who was in his twilight years and who meant a great deal to the person who made her very happy. Also, she figured that if she really set her mind to it, she could probably coax her father-in-law into at least a partial truce.

The last time we saw Carol, she was sporting a beautiful leather coat—a birthday gift from guess who? Her father-in-law.

What it boils down to is that not every woman will find fulfillment and happiness with a man in the same way.

The moral of these stories is very simple. There are some men who have special needs. Accepting those needs and acquiescing to them may seem at first to be retrogressive and unliberated. But isn't life in general a series of compromises, adjustments, and trade-offs? We are all seeking to attain our goals in life and love, and there is nothing wrong with reevaluating our priorities if that's what it takes to make it happen.

What may be comfortable and acceptable to one woman may not work for another! Keep an open and realistic mind in determining what will fulfill *your* needs, and don't think unkindly of someone else who may have different needs and different requirements for satisfying them.

Our seven rules for trading off in combination with your faithful adherence to the Venus formula may ignite a spark that turns your "trade off" into a real bargain!

SEVEN RULES FOR TRADING OFF

1. Calculate the difference between what you want in a man and what you actually *need* to make you happy.

2. Concentrate on what is right for you—not what your friends will think of your choice.

3. Never let him know he isn't the man of your dreams.

4. Give him the full benefit of the Venus formula.

5. Be sure the end justifies the means.

6. Use your charm to bring out the best in *him*.

7. Evaluate your life situation and decide what you are willing to sacrifice in order to get it.

14
Living Together...
A No-Win
Situation for You

It seems only a few years ago that young women wrote to advice columnists asking how to break the news to their parents that their roommates were of the opposite sex. It also seems like just yesterday that hostesses, friends, and families were asking how to address invitations and what to call the live-in loves.

Now it is rare not to know at least one live-in couple, and even the smallest town in mid-America has reluctantly accepted this fact of life. You may know people who rave about the merits of living together, but to be honest, we have never met a woman who particularly benefited from living together, and we have only known one such arrangement that lasted as long as a good marriage. Think about it: among your friends and acquaintances, how many live-together couples do you know who have lasted more than five years? We bet there aren't many.

But how many marriages can you think of that have lasted more than five years? More than ten years? Quite a few, most likely.

Our advice to women who want to be married is: don't be conned, convinced, or cajoled into a living-together arrangement. Marriage is a commitment. Living together isn't.

We've heard some real horror stories from women who tried it and sadly learned that their status legally and socially was no more than that of a close friend.

Elaine had been living with Dan for two years when he was rushed to the hospital from work with a severe heart attack. His boss called Dan's mother, Pearl, not Elaine, because his office records listed Pearl as next of kin. Pearl was naturally upset and didn't think of calling Elaine until after she had rushed to the hospital. By the time Elaine got there, Pearl had things organized. *She* decided which doctor to call. *She* filled out the admission forms. *She* was the one the doctors and nurses reported to. Elaine told us she felt like the invisible woman. Dan's mother was a very nice lady and liked Elaine, but when it came to an emergency, no one thought of Elaine's position. After all, Elaine wasn't his wife. She had no official status.

The final blow to Elaine's self-esteem came when she was refused admittance to the intensive care room—only family members were allowed. It was only after Elaine threw an unaccustomed tantrum that she was reluctantly allowed in to see Dan. When he was released three weeks later, Dan came home to Elaine, who was faced with the prospect of nursing him back to health.

Coping with a loved one's heart attack is difficult enough, but Elaine also had to struggle with the realization that she wasn't Dan's wife. She really had no position at all in the outside world. If, God forbid, Dan had died, there would have been no mention of her in the obituary, and only her closest friends would have known she was mourning. To the public, she was a nonperson.

Elaine's awakening came slowly but surely. She knew this arrangement was not for her. She was either going to be someone's wife again or she would be on her own, responsible only to herself. Never again would she accept this kind of limbo. As soon as Dan was out of danger, she told him how she felt and gave him the choice—marry her or lose her. Dan still couldn't make up his mind, so even though she loved him, Elaine packed up her things and left. She's sadder and wiser now, and she tries to get her message across to all her friends who seem to be heading for the same trap.

We have heard many variations of the same story from many different women. Brenda had been dating Shawn steadily for a year. They had rented an apartment together because Shawn wasn't ready for another marriage after his bitter divorce. At the wedding of Shawn's sister, the photographer posed the whole family together for a group shot. Shawn's sister Lila rounded up her parents, her sister and other brother, her brother's wife, their son, and Shawn. But she didn't invited Brenda to take part in the photo. She wasn't being mean; she just didn't consider Brenda family. She was just Shawn's girlfriend. Brenda watched the photographer take the photo with tears in her eyes and realized she literally wasn't in the picture with Shawn's family. The next day she told Shawn that living together was a mistake and she canceled the arrangement.

Sometimes living together does turn into marriage.

More often it doesn't. If a man is going to marry you, he will do it whether you live together or not. Actually, not only will living together make a man less likely to marry you, but it will also make him less willing to commit. And, after all, why should he? He has all the benefits of marriage and none of the responsibility. He has a permanent companion, full-time sex, a confidante, friend, housekeeper, hostess, expense sharer, and playmate—and he can leave at any time. It's true that the woman receives most of those benefits, too, but she also loses precious time. The longer she stays off the market, the harder it will be for her to find a new man. That's not true of the man. After the break-up, he can *always* find another willing woman. As we all know, a woman over fifty is considered "over-the-hill" by most men. But a fifty-year-old man is considered to be at his peak, particularly if he is successful. And women in their thirties hear their biological clocks loudly ticking away. Men in their thirties have no such alarms to spur them on to marriage. So keep in mind that, after the age of twenty-five or so, it's to a woman's great disadvantage to enter into any long-term live-in relationship if her ultimate goal is marriage.

We have met very few women, outside of movie stars, jet setters, or eccentrics who actually prefer living with their man in an unwedded state. Most women enter into such an arrangement for one of two reasons: either *she* suggests it because he won't commit to marriage and she hopes she can become indispensable to him and eventually convince him to marry her, or *he* suggests they try living together for a while "to see if it works out" because he won't commit to marriage. What a negative connotation those innocent-seeming words convey! People don't get married to see if it works out. People get married with joy and optimism, positive at that moment that it *will* work out. Didn't you? People who begin living together based on ifs are carrying a deadly amount of pessimistic baggage with them into the relationship. Instead of feeling security and happiness, they're acknowledging fear and caution. Quite an emotional difference!

"BUT WE CAN GET TO KNOW EACH OTHER BETTER"

We've all heard men claim they would never marry a woman without living together first because "you never know a person until you live with her." Don't fall for that line either. You can know each other just as well by spending lots of time together, sleeping together, cooking together, watching TV together, and taking trips together. You're not going to know each other any better by moving in together. In fact, you may not know each other as well.

Because you know it's a trial, each of you are making a greater effort to stay on your best behavior. Gena told us that all the time she was living with Bert, she never felt relaxed. If she was crabby or not feeling sexy or suffering one of her periodic migraines, a nagging fear crept in that maybe he would see that she was less than perfect and decide to end things. Ellen said that every time she and her live-in had a fight, she was afraid the relationship was over. Both women said they felt they were tiptoeing around the relationship and playing at love.

Conversely, as you know from your first marriage, little things you overlooked in him while you were playing at togetherness loom large and important once the knot is tied. We have known more than one couple who lived together for a couple of years, finally got married, and then separated a few months later. They all sang the same refrain: "I thought I knew him/her when we were living together. But after marriage, he/she changed into another person." They didn't change. Their expectations of each other changed, and they let down their guard with each other. The truth is, you will never really know another person until you *marry* him.

Living with another person is hard enough, anyway, but living together without the commitment of marriage is doubly difficult. When little annoyances and irritating habits crop up in marriage, most couples try to work things out; divorce is usually not the immediate solution. It takes time and effort to get divorced. But if you're only living together, it's too easy to just walk away from problems. It takes very little time and effort. There are no societal, familial, or legal pressures to stay and try to work things out; all you have to do is say goodbye.

Our wise friend Ann pointed out the most poignant difference we've heard between marriage and cohabitation: "Who celebrates the day you moved in together?" she asked. Your wedding anniversary is a date you will remember the rest of your life, even if you're subsequently divorced. But no one sends cohabitation anniversary congratulations, and how many live-ins or their friends and families remember the exact date the event took place years later?

WILL THERE BE A FUTURE?

Live-in couples rarely plan too far for the future because even though unspoken, both know there may not *be* a future. They don't burden themselves with too many expensive joint possessions for the same reason. We've known live-ins who have bought

homes together but who also drew a contract stipu-
lating who will buy out the other in case of a break-
up. What a negative way to embark on a romantic
adventure. Sure, married couples sometimes draw up
prenuptial agreements, too, but those are usually
older couples who have children from previous marriages to protect. (By the way, we don't believe in
prenuptial agreements, either, for the same reasons—
it focuses on divorce before you're even married.
Marvin Mitchelson, the famed Hollywood divorce
lawyer, once said on a TV program that he's never
known of a prenuptial agreement that didn't ultimately end in divorce. If you want to protect your
children, you can do it through wills or trusts.)

Married couples usually pool most of their income
figuring everything they do or buy is for "us." Live-ins
are usually quite careful about keeping accounts
separate and divvying up who pays for what. Again,
they're either consciously or unconsciously saying,
"We are not a unit, even in our own eyes." Deep in a
man's psyche, he does not feel the pride or protectiveness for his lover that he does for his wife.

If, after all the foregoing cautionary advice, you're
still determined to try living together in lieu of
marriage, at least have him move in with you. Then,
if it doesn't work out, you won't be the one to be
displaced. What a terrible feeling it must be to burn
all the bridges, give up your apartment or home,
move in with him, and then have nowhere to go if the
breakup comes.

Remember, you have neither law nor custom on
your side, so if the break comes, all you will salvage
is what you can negotiate. If you're living on his turf
and you have a nasty fight, he can literally turn you
out on the street, and you will have very little re-
course. Now, these are obviously worst-case scenar-

ios here, and it is possible that your relationship will never come to that. But it's best to be forewarned.

Maggie could talk for hours about worst-case scenarios. She is a Canadian and met Tony on a cruise. They had a long-distance romance for a few months, and eventually Tony asked her to move to California and live with him until they could get married. His reason for the delayed wedding bells was the new business venture he had just started; he wanted to devote his full energies to getting that off the ground before taking on the added commitment of marriage. But he assured Maggie it would be only a matter of time.

Maggie was afraid of losing Tony since they were a country apart, so she reluctantly agreed. She sold her home and car, gave up her teaching position, gave away or stored most of her possessions, and flew to Tony's arms. As a Canadian citizen she was only in the States on a visitor's permit, but she fully expected Tony to marry her before it ran out. A few months after they began their arrangement, Tony decided that he'd made a mistake. He really didn't want to get married after all.

Maggie was panic-stricken. She had foolishly given up everything to be with Tony. She had lost her seniority as a teacher, as well as most of her pension. She had no health insurance. She had no home or car left in Canada. She said she felt like a bag lady. Although she wanted to stay in California, it would be almost impossible for her to find a good job, let alone somewhere affordable to live. Friends urged her to see a lawyer, but Maggie knew that by the time the case was settled, the lawyer's fees would probably be higher than any settlement she would get. Besides, the courts no longer show much sympathy for a rejected woman. Maggie went back to Canada a sadder, wiser, and poorer woman, forced to pick up the pieces of her life and start all over again. That's why women must look out for themselves. If you're not going to take charge of your life, who is?

15
Nailing Down
the Commitment

We have talked about pursuing a successful relationship with a man from the moment of your initial contact with him. Your physical appearance, your assets and liabilities, your sex appeal, and your overall aura are all-important components in projecting that magic that will be irresistible to the man you want.

By now you should have a better understanding of why men are the way they are and how to appeal to their subconscious needs and drives. You should have a pretty good idea about what will bring him back after the first date. You can probably recognize men who send mixed signals. You know how to set the stage for your own seduction when *you* are ready for it (and how to make sure he'll come back for more). You know the importance of careful planning when the two of you go away together. And you should know which men are worth your time and

215

which aren't, and how to recoup if you forget to practice the Venus formula.

Let's assume you have done your homework, found the man you want, and worked your magic on him. Everything is progressing nicely . . . and progressing . . . and progressing. There comes a time in every relationship when it's time for the commitment to be made and the bond to be solidified—by a proposal of marriage—or it gradually drifts along, slowly stagnates, and then just fizzles out. Oh, sure, there are cases where a couple is together for years and then just finally decides to make it legal and everything works out fine. But in general, if marriage is your objective, the commitment should be nailed down before the dating pattern becomes too comfortable and easy.

You will instinctively know when you reach that point. You will sense when your relationship progresses from one stage to the next: you will have gradually increased the amount of time you spend together; your lives will have become more entwined; you will share more confidences with each other; you will have become an important part of each other's routines; you will think of yourselves as a couple; you will have become an essential part of your lover's life. He will be dependent on you. When you have reached that level and it continues at that level long enough for you to start feeling that the peak of the relationship has been reached, it is then time to pull out all the stops and zero in for the close.

In most situations, a year is plenty of time for a courtship. You are not going to know each other any better than you do after a year of exclusive togetherness until you get married and begin living together. Unfortunately, many women do find themselves in relationships that linger on and on, and show no signs of going anywhere. There are many things you can do to move the situation along, some as simple as explaining how you feel, others more elaborate. A friend of ours, Joan, reached this stage after almost a year of a very close and wonderful relationship with Joe, a man she wanted very much to marry. They had discussed marriage in an offhand way many times, and he usually made comments like, "When we're married, we'll sell your place and move into mine," and other vague references to tying the knot sometime in the future.

Joan is a very smart woman when it comes to dealing with men; she was a master of the Venus formula before we gave it a name. She knew if she came on too strong with Joe, he would back off and begin pulling away from her. But she was also quite certain that he loved her. So she decided to try a ploy that has worked in the game of love since the beginning of time: jealousy.

She mentally set a two-month time limit on her little deception, and then she set the stage. She started by acting somewhat distracted when she was with him. Oh, she was still caring and charming, but her manner and attitude were less intimate. She would make sure Joe caught her staring into space distractedly rather than into his eyes as she usually did, and then she would quickly and obviously double her attention toward him. She invented excuses for why she couldn't see him on various occasions. When he called to say goodnight at midnight, as was his routine when they weren't together, she often let her service pick up. The next day, she told him she must have fallen asleep early. She was eager and responsive during sex, just as she had always been, but again she held back just enough for him to notice the difference. After a couple of weeks, she sensed that he was beginning to wonder what was going on.

At the end of the third week, he asked her several times if anything was wrong, to which she answered (after a dramatic hesitation) that everything was fine; she just had a lot on her mind. Then she announced that she was going out of town for the weekend to visit a college friend who had just moved to a neighboring city. No, she said, he really wouldn't enjoy coming along; they had so much girl talk to catch up on. She would call him every day. Again she sensed that he was getting that feeling in the pit of the stomach that we are all familiar with: fear that something isn't right.

When she returned from her two days alone in the mountains during which she didn't call, Joe was angry and upset. She apologized profusely and said she had to talk to him that night. When he arrived at her home, she was calm and radiant. She wore his favorite outfit. She had his perfect martini waiting; she had prepared a wonderful dinner. She insisted he have his drink before they talked. When he had finished and she had refilled his glass, she sat down next to him, looked into his eyes, and dropped the bombshell.

She told him that she had met another man to whom she was very much attracted and that she had seen him several times over the last several weeks. She told him she was terribly confused because she knew she loved Joe, but the more time she spent with the other man, the more attracted she felt toward him, adding that he told her he cared enough to wait until she was ready—but he couldn't wait indefinitely. She went on to confess that she had spent her weekend away trying to decide what to do, because she felt she had to make a decision between the two men.

Joan almost was taken in by her own story. She said tears actually welled in her eyes. She then took Joe's hand and told him she now understood how difficult it must be for him to make the commitment to marriage because she was in a position of making a difficult decision herself. She put her arms around him and asked him to give her some time to decide what she should do.

Well, Joan said she had never seen him at a loss for words in the year they had been together. He was speechless. When she suggested they have dinner, he said he wasn't hungry and was going home to be alone and think about what had happened. She didn't hear from him for over a week, and she was scared to death that her radical plan had backfired. She knew she had taken a risk, but was certain that if she didn't do something drastic she would never see that wedding band on her finger.

Eight days after that evening, Joe called. She was warm, friendly, and vivacious on the phone, and when he asked to see her, she was enthusiastic. When they got together, he asked her what she planned to do. She sweetly told him that she would like to see both him and the other man for a while and see what happened. She also gave him the option of dating other women. He reluctantly agreed.

Joan kept up the pretense of seeing someone else for the next few weeks but was always caring and lovely when she was with Joe. She never questioned him about what he did when he wasn't with her. About a week before her mental deadline, she received two dozen roses with a card that said, "This is ridiculous. Let's get married next weekend if you're not already busy. Joe." She wasn't and they did.

When a man thinks he is in danger of losing someone he is hooked on, he will do whatever is necessary to keep that person—and that usually means marriage. Granted, Joan's plan was dramatic and could have backfired on another man, but she saw that when someone else wants something you have, it makes that person or thing even more important and precious. The idea that another man was interested in "*his*" woman, and that the interest might be mutual, has been the stimulus for many marches down the aisle.

We know you are probably thinking, "dishonesty, game playing, manipulation." We prefer to think of it as subtle persuasion. Much of what we do in life involves various types of subtle persuasion, as well as some game playing and manipulation. In our work, in our social contact with friends and relatives, in our day-to-day negotiations with others, we are always attempting to make things happen in a way that will be good for us. We try to convince others to see things our way, to do what we want them to do. There is nothing wrong with this. The person you are attempting to convince has the option of saying no and has the alternative of convincing you to do it his way.

So don't feel guilty about using your wits and imagination to get what you want. Remember, though, the manner in which you present your little drama is very important. If you are hostile, bitter, selfish, and demanding, the effect of anything you do will be lost. The secret of success in getting your way is to make it a win-win situation. Once you have what you want, make sure you give as much or more than you have gotten. In some cases, the end does justify the means—*if* it is a happy ending for both parties.

We found lots of cases where a little judicious jealousy put the zing back into a sluggish relationship. There is something a man finds exciting about being just a tiny bit unsure of the woman he loves. It will make him try harder to make you happy, and he will generally do whatever is necessary to keep you for himself. In other words, he'll marry you, if that's what you want.

Another friend had the presence of mind to turn an unexpected incident into a jealousy ploy. Sara and Kurt were engaged and were living together in her house prior to the wedding day. They had met soon after his separation from his wife of many years, and the divorce was not yet final. When his ex-wife found out that Kurt was really planning on remarrying, she had second thoughts about ending her marriage to him and asked to see him. She pulled out all the stops: they shared a history together, they could enjoy their grandchildren some day, they had so many shared memories. Poor Kurt was torn with guilt and indecision. He really did love Sara—she was the most wonderful woman he'd ever known—and the one thing he didn't share with his ex-wife was sex. It had been terrible between them for years. And it was wonderful with Sara.

On the other hand, he and his ex-wife did have children and history in common, and he believed strongly in family. He went home to Sara and told her what had happened. She was furious, and told him she wasn't going to wait around politely while he made up his mind. What about *her* feelings?

In the midst of this heated discussion, the phone rang. By a stroke of fate (or the hand of God) it was a previous lover of Sara's whom Kurt knew about. This man was more handsome, more successful, and richer than Kurt, and at one time he and Sara were a serious twosome. Out of the blue he was calling to tell Sara he had just broken up a two-year relationship and was thinking fondly of her.

Well, Sara summoned up all her acting skills and in a voice dripping with honey, began an intimate chat with him, laughing and cooing, while Kurt paced up and down in an agitated state. When she felt he had stewed long enough, Sara hung up and sweetly told Kurt that Bruce was calling to renew their old "friendship" and that perhaps that wouldn't be such a bad idea. She certainly wasn't going to sit around idle while he romanced his ex-wife. That scene did the trick, and they've been blissfully married for five years.

MAKING HIM JEALOUS

An effective way to give a man a dose of that green-eyed monster is to enlist the help of a male friend. It worked for Lois.

She had been going with Dale for over two years, with no plans for marriage. Every time she mentioned the subject he managed to come up with a dozen reasons why the time wasn't right. He was willing to live together, but she had enough sense to know that once he was settled into that comfortable (and un-committed) status, he would have no reason to change the arrangement. Lois knew that Dale loved her and considered her an important part of his life. But like many men, especially after one or two failed marriages, he was terrified of that final step. He needed something to jolt him into realizing how unhappy he would be without her.

Lois asked a long-time friend of hers if he would help her with her plan of action. All he had to do was call her at specified times when she knew Dale would be there to answer the phone. They would also go out to lunch occasionally (at her expense) to places where she knew they were likely to be seen by Dale's friends. She made arrangements with a florist to send her flowers once a week—delivered when she knew Dale would be there. It was expensive, but she felt it was worth the investment.

When Dale questioned her about the phone calls, the flowers, and the man with whom she had been seen lunching, she told him that, yes, this very charming man had been pursuing her and she had had a few innocent lunches with him because he was such an interesting person. But, of course, there was nothing more to it—she adored Dale. Yes, she admitted, he seemed to be quite taken with her and she *asked* him not to send any more flowers, but she did enjoy his company so much that she would like Dale to meet him and maybe they could all be friends.

Lois even went a step further. She invited Al, her coconspirator, to dinner at her house along with Dale. Al played his role to perfection. He was polite and charming to Dale and super-solicitous, complimentary, and overly attentive to Lois. She continued her ruse for a couple of months until for some miraculous reason Dale decided he had been single long enough. Naturally, Al was a guest at the wedding.

There are a few other techniques that also may do the trick.

You have probably heard of the classic sales adage: give your pitch, then shut your mouth and wait for the other person to speak. If you can remain silent and resist the urge to oversell, you will generally make the sale. This is harder than it sounds. The desire to fill the void of silence is very powerful, and it requires tremendous willpower to overcome it and wait.

Jill, a very successful saleswoman, told us that she used this method to get her husband to propose and that it was the hardest "close" she ever made. But it worked. They had been together on and off for several years. He had been in a very bad marriage and had told her from the beginning that he loved her but didn't want to marry again. The arrangement suited her for a while, but she eventually decided she wanted the emotional security and the total commitment of marriage.

This woman was one of the star salespersons in a very tough, competitive business. She knew how to market herself as well as her product. She knew from experience that convincing a person (whether it be a customer or a lover) to do what you want them to do involves making a good presentation, removing the objections, and making the close when the timing is right. She was convinced that her presentation was effective. She was certain that she satisfied Steve's needs on an emotional, intellectual, physical, and sexual level. She knew he felt comfortable and happy with her. She also felt she had done a good job of neutralizing the objections he had about marriage, which involved his wariness about women who were only out for his money (she had plenty of her own), his memories of women who were overly clinging and emotionally needy (she was neither), his disdain for women who were scatterbrained, sloppy, and disorganized (she was a perfectionist in all three areas). The relationship had reached a plateau, and she decided it was time for the close.

Jill asked Steve to a quiet restaurant where they could talk, since she had something important to discuss. She didn't broach the subject until they were finished with dinner and having their brandy. Then she straightforwardly laid it on the line.

First, she asked him if he was happy in the relationship. He said yes, that he had never been so happy with any woman, that everything was wonderful. She then asked if there was anything at all he would like to change about the relationship. He reiterated that he was supremely happy. She told him she felt the same way, and since they had been together happily for some time, shouldn't they either move to another level, or think about getting on with their lives separately? He was somewhat taken aback for a moment, but then he took her hand and said, "You're right, darling. Why don't you move in with me?" She smiled sweetly, withdrew her hand, looked into his eyes and said, "I don't live with a man unless I'm married to him." Then she shut her mouth, lit a cigarette, and waited, and waited, and waited.

Steve fidgeted, lit a cigarette, sipped his brandy, looked around the room, blew his nose, stared at her. The silence was agonizing, and although it was probably no more than a couple of minutes, she said it was the longest silence she ever endured. She admits that she actually bit her lip to keep from overselling. Finally he spoke, and his words were the ones she wanted to hear: "Well, I guess we should get married then."

If Jill had reiterated all of her reasons for wanting to get married, rambled on about how wonderful it would be, and allowed herself to be drawn into a debate about the pros and cons of doing it, the issue would have become controversial, and he would have spent the rest of the evening in conversation avoiding a definite decision.

SHOCK THERAPY

Another method of getting a commitment from a gun-shy man is what we call shock therapy.

Pamela figured this out without ever reading it in a

book. She and Roy had been dating steadily for seven or eight months. They had met around the time she was thinking of moving to another city, where she had already arranged to share an apartment with two other women. When she met Roy, a confirmed bachelor sought after by every single woman in town, they had instant rapport, and the relationship developed very quickly. So she decided to put off her move for a few months and see what happened. Well, the romance continued to sizzle and Roy seemed crazy about her. But he never mentioned marriage. Pamela loved him, but she was determined not to sit around waiting from him to make a decision. Besides, after one failed marriage, she didn't have any more time to waste. She wanted to marry Roy and start a family or move to the other city and get on with her life.

New Year's Eve was coming up. She splurged on a fantastic red taffeta Marilyn Monroe type dress—strapless and tight—which was totally out of character for her. She got a new hairdo, took special pains with her makeup, and used every possible way to make Roy feel extra special all evening. It was a fantastic, magical night.

When they got back to her apartment, they made love, and she made sure it was an all-time great for him. Afterward when they were cuddling, she calmly told him that this had been their last night together. She said she loved him very much, and she had hoped he loved her, too, but apparently he didn't feel the same way she did. She said she realized he wasn't ready for marriage and that she understood, that it was okay, and that she hoped they could be friends.

He tried to negotiate for more time but she held firm. They both cried a little, and he left.

For the next three days she disappeared to a friend's

house (by prearrangement). He called everyone trying to find her (including the friend she was with,
who covered for her). After she went home on the
fourth day, a few more days passed, and she didn't
hear from him. She started packing, figuring she had
given it her best shot and lost. Of course, he finally
showed up and proposed. That was ten years ago, and
she says he still won't let her get rid of that red
taffeta dress.

THE TANTRUM

Some men respond better to blatant outrage than
they do to subtle persuasion. If this is your situation,
you might want to consider throwing a judicious
temper tantrum—once, and only once, to get your
point across.

Peter had promised marriage twice to Amy. Each
time he had changed his mind the next day. Once he
had even left her to go back to a former lover, and
another time he suddenly stopped seeing Amy for a
month. Each time, of course, he came back professing
his love and devotion. Amy would not have put up
with this treatment except that she knew Peter really
had good instincts and was a kind and decent man—
with a serious fear of commitment. She knew he
would be a wonderful, loyal husband if he could get
over his fears. She also knew that his mother, to
whom he was devoted, had a hot temper when she
was crossed. Amy observed that Peter seemed even
more loving after the few times she had lost *her*
temper.

In desperation, Amy decided she would have to
assert herself with Peter in one final explosion to
extract a marriage commitment. If she lost then, she

would say good-bye to him permanently.

She actually practiced acting out her anger until she was comfortable with it. She pounded her pillow, swatted tennis balls with all the strength she could muster, and practiced shouting into the mirror. Then she waited for the right moment to confront Peter.

She used his coming home too late one night as a pretext for her indignation. She angrily accused him of cheating on her, of not loving her, and of not taking her feelings seriously. She worked herself up into such a good rage that she was actually enjoying it! She stood there in her skimpy teddy (Peter loved sexy lingerie) pouting and raging and telling Peter that they were through. How dare he treat her like this? She was too good for him. Peter, of course, was taken aback and tried to cajole her and calm her down. But nothing would quiet Amy. She finally threw a couple of books and wine glasses at the wall (being careful not to hit Peter), tossed a few more choice phrases over her shoulder, flounced out of the room into the bedroom, and locked the door.

Peter pounded on the door, begging her to be reasonable, professing his love for her. Finally, after a few more minutes of turmoil, he shouted that he loved and wanted to marry her.

Amy flung open the door and fell into Peter's arms. But she refused to have sex with him until he called his mother and announced their engagement. His mother was crazy about Amy. She knew he'd never back out once he went that far, or he'd have to face his mother's temper.

Now this tactic might seem a bit extreme, and we wouldn't advise most women to use it, but Amy knew her man. Our theory is, use whatever works to get that marriage proposal.

THROWING HIM OFF BALANCE

Sometimes just throwing the man off balance by acting in a way that surprises him will get the desired results.

This was the case with Laura. It was the same old story: she had been going with Dean for over a year, and he was scared to death of taking that final step to the altar. It finally got to the point where he knew he had to make a decision. So he did what a lot of people do when they don't want to make a decision: he ignored the situation—and Laura. He just stopped calling one day. She didn't hear a word from him for three weeks.

Laura should win an award for self-discipline because she never picked up the phone to call him. She sat it out. Of course, she was quite certain he loved her and sensed that he wanted to cement the relationship, but that he had the emotional block from which many men suffer. When he finally did call, he acted as if nothing had happened, and so did Laura. She was warm, charming, friendly, and sounded as if she was delighted to hear from him. He later told her he was shocked: he expected her to be either angry, hostile, and accusatory, or cool, distant, and hurt. He certainly didn't expect her to sound as if she hadn't even realized it had been three weeks since he called! They got together the next night, and she was so charming and attentive you would have thought it was their first date! He decided that any woman who had that much style was too good to let get away and that he had better convince her to marry him. To this day, he probably believes *he* convinced *her*.

As we've said before, men like to do the chasing. They still like to feel they are the dominant force in a relationship, the leader and protector. There are some instances, however, when a man just needs to be told straight and simply that it's time to get married—and with a certain kind of man, it is just that simple.

This was the case with Sandra, a wonderful interior decorator. She met Ben at a friend's party. He was a recent widower who had just moved into a condo and mentioned to Sandra that he was having trouble decorating it. Sandra found Ben to be very attractive and wanted to get to know him better, so she offered to take a look at the condo and give him an idea of what it would cost to decorate it.

She found out from her friend that Ben had been happily married for twenty years and hadn't really been dating much since his wife died. But once she began work on his condo, one thing led to another and they started going together on a regular basis. They got along beautifully and everyone thought of them as a couple. Ben was happy to have her handle all the social plans. His wife had always done that, and he expected it, so he was completely accustomed to complying with a woman's suggestions. After ten months, Sandra decided if she didn't take the initiative, Ben would be content to drift along in limbo indefinitely. She knew he was very relaxed and comfortable in their relationship and that he was very happy with her. She also knew and understood his nature, which tended to be somewhat preoccupied and passive.

One night at dinner, she just very sweetly said, "Darling, we've been together for almost a year. I think it's time we got married." Ben's response was, "Gee, has it been only a year? I feel like I've known you forever. Of course we'll get married, been thinking of that myself."

So you see, you have to know your man and what makes him tick. Some men don't even need subtle persuasion; they just need to be asked.

The last chink in a man's armor is usually dissolved when you find his hidden key and fill that need. In Ben's case, it was continuing the same routine that he had found comfortable in his long, happy marriage. With some men, it is boosting their egos in an area where it is lacking. In others, it is satisfying their desire to be mothered, or stimulating their territorial instincts by provoking jealousy, or accepting their drive to be a nurturer.

The best way to find a man's hidden key, as we pointed out earlier, is to draw out his innermost feelings and emotions. If you can somehow convince a man that he can safely share his true feelings with you without losing stature or being judged, you will have won half the battle.

Whatever the key to his emotional dependence may be, if you find and fulfill that need, you will become indispensable to him, and he will think making that ultimate commitment was *his* idea all along.

When it's time to nail down the commitment, remember these guidelines for what does and doesn't work:

DOES WORK:

- Make him think it's his idea.

- Don't let the relationship drift for too long.

- Let him be aware that you are desirable to other men.

- Make him part of your social circle.

- Hold back just enough to keep him guessing.

- Make sure his friends and family like you.

DOESN'T WORK:

- Nagging
- Begging
- Crying
- Reasoning
- Logic
- Arguing
- Guilt
- Accusations

Above all, remember that a commitment is not a commitment until a wedding date is set and publicly announced. Vague promises of marriage sometime up the road are just that, vague promises. A *real* commitment means setting a date, time, and place, and making the announcement to friends and family.

16
The Ultimatum . . . What Do You Have to Lose?

Ultimatum: "*A final proposition or demand, one whose rejection will end negotiation and cause . . . direct action.*"
(Webster's New Collegiate Dictionary)

We must tell you upfront that the ultimatum is absolutely the last technique to be used in your campaign to land your man. Use it only after you have tried every other conceivable ploy to get your commitment. Only use the ultimatum if: (1) you are prepared to stick to it and not back down, and (2) you are prepared to walk away if it does not work.

Do not use the ultimatum as a threat. Do not plan to give in if it doesn't work. Unless you can psyche yourself up to do or die, don't use the ultimatum, because it will only backfire, leaving you in a weaker position than before. You can use it only if you are dealing from a position of inner strength. If there are any doubts in your mind or manner when you issue your ultimatum, your man will sense it and you will lose your advantage. He's got to know you mean it. He has to be convinced that you are absolutely at the end of your rope and that you are prepared to walk away from him forever. He's got to believe that there will be no more second chances, no more "just a little while longer." This is it. Ground zero. He won't believe it unless you do.

Issuing an ultimatum is like playing a strategy game. You must state your terms, remain firm in your position, and turn away all objections. You must not under any circumstances negotiate or deviate from your stated objective. You state your position, say what the consequences will be if you don't get what you are asking for, and set a time limit for action to be carried out.

Your man will have one of several reactions: disbelief, anger, hurt, argument, laughter, reason. He probably won't believe you're serious, and depending on his nature, he'll throw a tantrum, leave in a sulk, try to humor you, or reason with you. *You must pay no attention to any of these reactions.* Do not let him goad you to anger or long justifications of your position. If he leaves temporarily, just repeat your ultimatum when he returns. Pretty soon it will sink in that you actually do mean what you are saying and that he will have to deal with it. Do not give him too long to come to his decision.

Depending on your feel for the situation, you might negotiate the time limit with him. That way, you leave him some breathing room. But don't leave him too much room. A week is maximum. You want to stay in charge of this situation. You want to keep the pressure on.

Pam was getting increasingly dissatisfied with Gordon's vacillating about marriage. They had been together for three years, and she felt the relationship was stagnating and she just couldn't go on this way any longer. She thought long and hard about the pitfalls of issuing an ultimatum until she was sure that if she couldn't be Gordon's wife, she wanted to wipe the slate clean and get on with her life without him. She knew that nagging, reasoning, or crying wouldn't work (it never does). But she also knew that with Gordon, shouting or anger would be equally counterproductive. So she decided on the soft but firm stance.

She set the stage carefully and rehearsed her speech. After a leisurely candlelight dinner (at which she purposely held back on the wine), she told Gordon there was something she had to talk to him about. She sat them both on the couch, took Gordon's hand, and told him she had made an unalterable decision to end their relationship unless he was willing to marry her. Of course, Gordon didn't take her seriously. After all, he had heard this from her before.

He went through the usual objections and gave the usual excuses. Pam quietly waited until he was through, then said that this time was different. Her mother was coming to visit three weeks from today, and she would like to have the wedding during her stay. Just a quiet family affair.

Gordon was getting more and more uncomfortable and mumbled that he needed time to think about it. Pam remained calm and pleasant and asked him how much time he needed. Gordon didn't know. Pam said that a week from today should be enough time. If by then he could not see his way clear to marrying her, then, much as she loved him, their affair was over forever. She also told him not to call or see her until he had come to his decision.

Before this conversation could escalate into an all-night marathon of discussion, Pam asked Gordon to leave. By this time they were both ready to cry. But she stood firm. At the door they kissed and clung to one another as though they could never part. Emotions were at a high pitch. As soon as Gordon left, Pam collapsed in a heap of tears and turned on her answering machine.

Of course, Gordon called her an hour later and an hour after that. Pam refused to answer. She instructed her secretary at the office not to put Gordon's calls through, and she didn't return his messages. On the third day, he was waiting outside her door as she left for the office, begging to talk to her. Pam just calmly asked if he had made his decision yet. When Gordon couldn't answer, she said just as calmly that they had nothing to talk about and left.

On the fourth day, Pam didn't hear from him at all. On the fifth day, a balloon was delivered to her office with a note: "Call your mother and invite her to a wedding. I love you. Gordon."

Pam later told us she had never been through such an agonizing emotional experience in her life. But she was prepared to see it through. Gordon said that he, too, had gone through an emotional wringer. But the thought of losing Pam was more unbearable than his fear of commitment.

Don't try the ultimatum unless you have a strong stomach and heart, because you are playing for very high stakes. Your emotions, as well as his, are on the line. On the other hand, if the relationship is going nowhere and marriage is your goal, then what do you have to lose? Only another precious few years of your life!

Issuing an ultimatum doesn't always work, so if you can get your man to commit by any other means, do that first. Most men are stubborn and don't like to be dictated to, so the ultimatum may have the opposite effect of driving away a man who really wants you. Also, never use the ultimatum unless you are sure you know what gets to him emotionally. If you are certain that you are emotionally indispensable to him and that losing you would be more painful to him than marrying you, then an ultimatum may do the trick.

Nita used this tactic on Peter, her live-in of two years. Peter had been vacillating about marriage—one minute sure of it and the next minute backing away. Nita was at the end of her patience and growing increasingly short-tempered. She knew their relationship was deteriorating under the strain anyway, and she made up her mind that she would rather live without Peter than live with uncertainty any longer.

Nita stayed home from work one day, packed up all Peter's clothes, had the locksmith change the locks on the doors (luckily it was her house), made Peter a reservation at a nearby Holiday Inn, sent his suitcases there, and left a note on the door. Then she called Peter at his office, warned him that she had taken direct action, wished him well and hung up before he could say anything.

Her note to Peter told him how much she loved him and asked him not to get in touch with her unless he was willing to set a wedding date. Then she left town for a week. In this case, the ultimatum didn't work. Peter still wouldn't commit. But at least Nita now knew that the relationship was not as deep as she had thought, and she stuck to her decision to make a new life without Peter.

Another woman we know bought two tickets to Paris and told her lover she was taking them on a honeymoon. All he had to do was show up at City

Hall the day before the flight so they could get married. If he didn't show up, she told him, she was planning to go to Paris anyway. He showed up with a bottle of champagne and a diamond wedding ring.

Sometimes a major life change will force a commitment. You can announce a job transfer to a distant city. You have to make a decision whether or not to sell your house and move into an apartment big enough for only one. Your lease is up and you must move. Are you going to move alone or together? Your married daughter wants to move in with you. Your mother wants you to move in with *her*.

There's an axiom in business that you might keep in mind: the more time, money, and energy a man puts into a relationship, the more likely he is to be committed to it, and the less likely he is to walk away. Most men don't like to lose an investment.

The ultimatum is not for everyone. Don't use it unless you have exhausted all other means of getting a commitment. Even the best planned ultimatum might not work, but if you have nothing else to lose, why not try it?

Your Turn

Now it's time for you to put our advice into practical action. We know that we have made some controversial statements and that it may be difficult for many women to accept some of our suggestions, but believe us, they work. Some of the techniques we employ in this book may seem to be manipulative, and in a way, some are. But almost everything in life involves manipulation and compromise. However strange these techniques may seem, and even though you may have to force yourself to practice them at first, they will be worth the good, warm, loving relationship you will soon be enjoying with your new husband.

Just think of the powerful forces that are manipulating us every day of our lives. Advertising, the media, political candidates, bosses, friends, lovers, parents, and children—all trying to win us over to their point of view, to buy their product, or to do things their way.

So, in order to compete in the love game, you must employ some of the same strategy. At all times we strive for a win-win situation in which you both get what you want.

Love is the most important force in life. Career, money, power, prestige, accomplishment, recognition, are all wonderful ideals to strive for. But even those fortunate enough to attain all those goals still fall in love and marry, often more than once. Human beings are incredible optimists.

Love is the elixir of life, the moving force of the universe. But there is no sense in merely thinking about and wishing for love. You must make it happen to you.

We want you to find a good man to share your life with, someone with whom you can share the love you are so ready and willing to bestow on him. We wish you well and we know that you will succeed in beating the odds and finding lifelong love and commitment.

Good luck!

P.S. We want to hear from you. Please write and tell us how this book has affected your life.

Teddi Sanford and Mickie Silverstein
8217 Beverly Blvd.
Los Angeles, CA 90048